ENTITLED TO NOTHING

BOB WALSH

Hop –

Keep chopping away out there brother. Hoping you can use a quick off-season read. Always rooting hard for you.

Win Anyway,

Bob Walsh

To Lefty and Bitsy

For your unconditional love, your unwavering support, and your generous spirit…

I can never thank you enough.

CONTENTS

FOREWORD

When I showed up on the campus of Providence College in the fall of 2002, I didn't really understand how to get better. I loved basketball and I was pretty good at it, but I didn't have a plan to improve. I generally did what was comfortable to me and stuck to the things I was good at.

I was originally going to redshirt my freshmen year, so I didn't have to worry about playing in the games. That meant a lot of extra time in the gym before and after practice with Coach Walsh. At that point, I couldn't foresee the impact that time would have on me personally or as a basketball player.

Coach Walsh helped me see the value in opportunity. The opportunity to dedicate myself and to truly commit to getting better. His leadership helped me to create an identity, one that was more than just as a basketball player. It helped me fall in love with the process of improvement, and the little things that were a big part of it. It was a daily commitment to practice habits, to the approach. Coach Walsh would never let me make excuses, and he showed me that effort level was my choice, not something that could be taught.

On those days when it was just the two of us in the gym, I realized it didn't have to be work. If I really loved basketball the way I said, it was a commitment to something I loved. It was obvious how much Coach Walsh loved being in the gym – leading, coaching, teaching – so it didn't feel like work, as much as we were just making each other better.

He had a voice that I needed to consistently hear. He delivered the message directly, and I always knew I was getting the truth. In fact, he made me comfortable hearing the truth. I recognized the value Coach Walsh brought to my approach. He made me hungry for improvement. When I was in the gym by myself or back home for a break, I'd still hear his voice. Are you going hard enough? Is that good enough? Push yourself, Gomes. Don't leave anything in the tank.

Those days he would always be the first one in the office – running his miles on the treadmill, watching the film of practice. Then he would scout our next opponent, get on the floor early with guys, run the scout team and lead defensive drills in practice. And after everyone left, he'd say, "You ready, three?" and he'd grab a ball and we'd get to work. He showed me what leadership, commitment, and determination were all about, because he lived it every day. He was the best example of how I could separate myself by investing in the process.

He helped build me. He taught me to ask the right questions of myself, to create personal growth. He made sure I never made excuses. He showed me a path to elite performance, one I was able to sustain through my four years at Providence College and nine more years in the NBA.

I'm grateful for the values instilled in me through his leadership. I'm also grateful for our friendship and connection that carries on today. I'm so excited for this book, so you all can get the insights that had such an impact on me as a player and a person.

Thank you, Coach Bizzle, for the leadership that inspired this young kid to achieve.

Always love,

RG3

Ryan Gomes

WHAT PEOPLE ARE SAYING

Bob Walsh is a program builder. I coached division III basketball in New England, and what Bob was able to do at Rhode Island College was incredible. Anyone can build a team but building a program that has sustained success takes great leadership and that is what Bob was able to build.

Stan Van Gundy, Head Coach, New Orleans Pelicans

With practical insights on team building and leadership, *Entitled to Nothing* is a must read for the leader of any organization seeking a practical guide for achieving competitive advantage, performance improvement and the realization of individual and team potential.

Phil O'Brien, Managing Partner, The York Consulting Group, LLC

Coach Walsh is a must read and must listen for me. He understands that leadership is not one thing and it's never figured out. Bob has been a great resource for me in considering new ways to think about the issues all leaders encounter.

Craig Counsell, Manager, Milwaukee Brewers

Coach Walsh shares practical lessons of leadership from his career as a college basketball coach that are in full need within corporate leadership development programs today. Learning to listen to your front line, building trust and confidence, creating buy-in to the vision, and working to transform a culture are just a few of the key lessons contained within this read. Any leader with these priorities will find great value in this book.

Tony Dottino, President, Dottino Consulting Group

INTRODUCTION

AN UNCOMMON APPROACH TO LEADERSHIP

On the day I was introduced as the head basketball coach at Rhode Island College in September of 2005, I walked up the steps of the Murray Center headed toward my press conference. I was stopped by a student who introduced himself as Kevin Payette, a senior on the basketball team. School had already been in session for two weeks when I was hired, so the team had returned to school without a head coach.

KP handed me a calendar and said "This is our schedule for workouts, lifting and conditioning. Good luck at the press conference, I look forward to talking to you afterwards." I thanked him and walked into the building pretty impressed. The players had been running the program on their own in the absence of a head coach. I didn't know it at the time, but I had just met my first captain.

That day, when I became a head coach for the first time, was also the day I started a master class in leadership development. Like most assistant coaches I had prepared diligently for that moment. I had all the ideas about how we were going to play, what we were going to run on offense, how we would attack on defense and all of the tactical moves I would use to win basketball games. What I didn't know was that all of it would add up to maybe 25% of my job as a head coach. The majority of my focus would be leadership. It would be learning how to get a group of people aligned to critical behaviors that led to successful outcomes. Coaching was more about leadership than I had realized.

I knew that leadership was important. I had grown up as the captain of most of the teams I played on and I started coaching when I was a junior in college. All good teams needed effective leadership. But I had never actually studied leadership, I just figured you either had it or you didn't. I took it for granted, as if it was this organic mindset that took over within a team. I never recognized the impact it had on success, or the fact that it could be taught and developed. I would learn to see leadership as a skill and not a rank.

Every day I spent building the program at Rhode Island College was a day in a leadership classroom. I learned that culture – the behavior that resulted from a shared set of beliefs – was the key to success, and the environment I created was the most important part of my job. Our culture was built entirely on our process, the commitment we made to what we did each day, independent of the result. While I originally provided the direction as the head coach, as we learned what it took to sustain success, I understood our players needed to own the process and the results. The culture had to be theirs, not mine.

This the story of a basketball dynasty built at Rhode Island College, an NCAA division III state school located in Providence, Rhode Island. It's a look inside how a championship culture was built, and the leadership lessons learned and applied within that culture. By creating the right environment, we were able to establish a mentality and change behaviors with an approach that not only won a lot of basketball games but had a significant impact on the lives of everyone involved. I'm forever grateful to be a part of that group.

When I became a head coach, I thought my job was basketball. I learned quickly it was actually to lead, and basketball was simply the teaching tool. My arena happened to have two baskets and a scoreboard. Your arena may be an executive boardroom, a classroom, a conference center or a factory. While the context of our situations might be different, the lessons learned are universal and can be applied to any organization. It is a foundation for success in any walk of life.

This is the story of an uncommon approach to leadership.

ONE

BECOMING A LEADER

SEPTEMBER 2005

J ack Perri was definitely surprised to hear my voice. I had just finished my seventh year as an assistant coach at Providence and I'd heard the rumor that he was leaving Rhode Island College after one year as their head coach to join Jim Ferry's staff at LIU as an assistant. It was the middle of August, not exactly the time of year when there is much movement in the coaching business. At first, he was surprised I'd heard the news, as he definitely didn't want it public just yet. But he was even more surprised when I told him I was interested in the job, that I wanted to know what it was like to coach at RIC. I could sense the confusion, the "Why is a Big East assistant calling me about my job?" in his voice. The campuses of Providence and RIC are only about one mile away from each other, but as basketball programs they are on different planets.

I loved being an assistant in the Big East, but after seven years I wanted the challenge of being a head coach. Having attended a division III school myself – Hamilton College in Clinton, NY – I had a good idea about that level. I knew most of the players had a genuine love for the game, and there was something very pure about the approach. I felt it was time to take everything I had learned and

1

build my own team. I was thrilled when Don Tencher, the athletic director at RIC, called and offered me the job.

I hadn't met any of the players when I showed up for the press conference, Don told me he'd have the team ready for a meeting right afterwards. Walking into the Murray Center and meeting KP was my first lesson in leadership. This team was about to meet their third head coach in as many years, and they came back to school without knowing who that coach would be. But they were running everything themselves. They were forced to take ownership of the program, and they did. I had a good feeling about my new team before I even met them.

Listen More, Say Less

After the press conference, I met with the team in a classroom in the Murray Center. That meeting is always a challenge, especially when it's your first time in charge. The kids wanted to know who I was and what I was all about. And I was dying to tell them. But I wanted to listen more than talk. I resisted the temptation to talk about myself and made it a point to listen to them. I think seeing KP before the press conference when he handed me that schedule altered my approach. I needed to learn about the program, the players, and the culture. I needed to understand the personalities of the individuals and the team. Your first day as a leader feels like it is supposed to be about you, but it's really about the team in front of you.

It might be the biggest challenge you face when taking over a new organization – you want to make an impact and instill your culture right away. You can see what the program is going to look like, and you can't wait to get it there. But it requires patience and mental discipline. You have to listen to your players and learn about them before you can get them to buy-in to your beliefs. Effective leadership is about listening more than talking, especially early on as you establish relationships.

A culture is built over time through daily action and approach. It's a brick by brick scenario. And haven't we always been taught that a great leader is the guy in the front of the room, telling everyone what the plan is? Well, I learned on my very first day that listening is one of the most powerful weapons in leadership. And the knowledge you need to build your organization the right way comes from the people you are trying to lead. Your connection with them is more important than your ideas about how to build your program.

That day, I started to understand a truth I would come to believe in strongly as a head coach. I learn the most about my team—and we are at our best—when I am listening to my players. The standard model of coaching—with the leader in the front of the room telling everyone what to do—isn't the most effective model. It isn't the best way to get the most out of your team. Talk to your people. Ask them questions. They may not always tell you what you want to hear, but they will tell you what you need to know.

Create the Space for Ownership

One afternoon, about a week later, I was cleaning my new office when Kevin Payette came in. KP would be the only senior on my first team and our captain. Not only did I benefit from having a very good team—looking back, I think we were the best team in the league my first year—but we also had only one senior, and he was a terrific leader. The combination of talent and leadership made things much easier on a first year head coach.

KP was sitting in the office and talking to me about our pre-season pickup games. I had gone recruiting the day before, so I hadn't seen the guys when I normally would as they came over to play. I asked KP how the games went.

"Ah, not very good. They were kind of bullshit. Guys weren't playing hard, guys were complaining. It wasn't good at all."

I figured I'd put it on him and see how he responded. "Really? What are we going to do about it?" I wasn't really expecting an answer, but I figured we could start a conversation about how to fix the issue.

His answer surprised me. "We already took care of it. We got up at 7 AM this morning and ran as a team. Everybody came in and ran. The guys know we can't have that."

I tried not to let him see my surprise. I asked the question pretty confident that I wasn't going to get a good answer other than, "I don't know, coach. If guys don't play hard, I'm not really sure what we can do." But he had taken ownership along with the rest of the team for some garbage pickup games in the pre-season. This wasn't something I had stressed to them. This was something they had done on their own. They had standards for how they should compete, even in the pre-season, and they held themselves accountable to those standards. That said a lot about the team I was now coaching.

How many teams are getting up before class and running to punish themselves for bad pickup games? I was impressed. It showed me for certain that these kids cared. They wanted to be good, and they took it seriously. It also showed me that they would take responsibility and ownership, which is important in any successful organization. So often as leaders we want to correct mistakes and tell people what to do. In reality, high performing teams are driven from the inside out. I got my first glimpse of that lesson in the office with KP that day. Our job as the leader is not to tell them what to do, but to give them the tools to figure it out themselves. I wanted my team to be full of leaders, not followers. They had the space to take ownership when their coach left right before school. I'd learn over time to continue to give them that space.

There is a big difference between a team being told what to do and doing it on their own. Compliant teams will do what they are told, and with talent they can be good. Teams that take ownership do it for each other, and those teams have a chance to be special. When they own it, they'll fight a little harder for it. When your team starts to drive your culture, elite success is more attainable.

Taking ownership became an important part of the championship culture we built at Rhode Island College and it started when they were in the gym as a team, on their own. And it became a big part of what we did because of the kids we had. I was a first year leader and they showed me that they were willing to take ownership. I learned the value of that from my players. When I left the office that night a building block for our culture had been set, even if I didn't know it at the time.

When No One Is Watching

The pickup games became a very important part of our culture as well. College basketball teams usually play three or four days per week in the pre-season. Different programs place different levels of importance on them. Some take them seriously, others don't care, some don't play much pickup at all. Many coaches just accept that the pickup games are going to be bad and there isn't much you can do about it, but that always struck me as odd. If it was something our team was going to do a lot—and they may play more pickup basketball together than any other activity—than we should make sure they take it seriously. If they spent a lot of time doing it, it was counterproductive to let them develop bad habits. I knew when I took over my own program, I was going to make pickup games a priority.

Within any organization, you are always going to have your own "pickup" games. What are your people doing together when the leadership isn't watching? That's essentially what pickup games are to college basketball programs. Time spent by the people in your organization working on their skill set when the leadership isn't around. And I'm sure it's happening a lot, regardless of the field. Figure out what your organization's pickup games are, and make sure they matter. Your approach will impact your personnel even when you aren't present, and that time spent together will impact your organizational culture. If your people are going to be doing something a lot, it's going to have an impact on your results. Make sure they are doing it right.

I wanted to place an emphasis on our pickup games. I thought it was important, but I had no idea how important. Those games became something our players took ownership of from day one in the fall, and it established a level of ownership that was requisite to be a part of our team. Due to NCAA rules, we weren't allowed to coach our players in the pre-season. They were on their own, and whether I knew it or not our culture was being established.

A lot can be learned about the leadership of an organization by observing the team when the leadership isn't present.

Questions Create Alignment

Like most aspects of our culture, the first key with our pickup games was the kids. We had kids who loved to play, kids who played hard, and kids who were tough. Giving them ownership was pretty easy. I wanted to provide the structure they needed but still make it theirs. I started to discover the value of asking questions.

After talking with KP, I asked the players in an informal meeting about the pickup games. Did they think they were good enough? Should they be better? Did we need to do something different? There was a consensus – some days the games were good, some days they were bad. They weren't consistent, and they definitely needed to be better. I asked them if they thought the games were important, and they all said yes. They were playing four days a week for almost two hours at a time. If we were going to invest that much time in it, should we make sure we do it the right way? They all agreed. They wanted to change the way we played pickup.

I learned that asking questions of my players really helped my development as a leader. It started us down the road of developing real trust. Asking questions creates alignment, and alignment creates a safe space for change and growth. When you come across the inevitable difficult times, you can circle back to your questions and reinforce your alignment. This strengthens the trust within your team when you need it the most. You can never ask too many questions.

The players felt like I valued their opinion, and it allowed them to take more ownership. There's an old adage that applies to leadership "If I say it, you doubt it. If you say it, it's true." By asking them questions about the pickup games I was giving them freedom to establish what needed to change. And perhaps more importantly, I wasn't coming in and laying down the law. Lao Tzu said, "To lead people, walk beside them," and that's what I was doing. I didn't want to be the new coach who had all of the answers and blamed any lack of success on them. Asking questions created alignment, ownership, and trust, while showing them a pathway towards meaningful change.

The whole team agreed that the pickup games were important and that they needed to change. My next question was "What can we do about it?" Again, I allowed them to take some responsibility and give feedback. Then I was able to give some suggestions. "How about if we brought some structure to it? How about if we made all of the games more competitive? Do you think you guys can handle that?"

We talked it out and came up with a structure:

- Each week we'd pick three teams, and everyone stayed on the same team for the week.
- The players would count the wins and losses each day, and the team at the end of the week with the most losses would get up and run a timed mile on Monday morning. This made the games very competitive. No one wanted to run on Monday, and guys took great pride in never being on the team that had to run.
- Games were straight to seven, with no three pointers. Everything was a point. We didn't want the games to run

too long and get lazy, and we wanted to avoid arguments about a shot being a two or three. I also wanted to encourage guys to get to the rim.

- On the seventh point, the scorer had to make a free throw to win the game. If you missed the free throw the bucket didn't count and you played the rebound live. The game continued.

- If the offense scored a basket and all five offensive players hadn't crossed half court, the basket didn't count, the ball was turned over to the defense. If the offense scored a basket and all five defensive players hadn't crossed half court, the bucket counted, and the offense got the ball back. This forced players to run hard and play every possession.

- The offense was not allowed to call fouls. All fouls were called by the defense. There's no stopping after a contested shot so people would just assume you got fouled. If the defense fouls somebody, they call it. If there is no foul called, keep playing. This is perhaps the most important and most challenging rule. You certainly need buy-in from your leaders, but it goes a long way to developing trust. You might think there were a lot of arguments over fouls with this process, but the opposite was the case. Everyone knew they couldn't stop and assume a foul would be called. You had to play through it.

The more we talked about our pickup games, the more excited the guys got about them. It may seem like a lot of structure, but it was theirs, even though I had provided some suggestions. They owned it, and when they played, they knew I wouldn't be there. They had to execute the plan.

Take a close look at your organization and figure out when your team is playing their pickup games. Look at your weekly staff meetings. How do you engage your team to create alignment? How do you encourage them to take ownership and use their personality to flourish? Are you making statements to them or are you asking them questions? I'd be willing to bet that much of your organization's productivity happens when you aren't in the room, when they are playing their own pickup games. They are working hard to make your team successful when they are alone or in small groups. Ask them questions and find out what needs to improve, and what you can do to help. You can give them input and you'll always be able to go back to their statements on getting better. Most importantly, when they figure out their new approach, get out of the way and let them execute it. In the long run you will get much more production out of them.

I never could have imagined how important those pre-season pickup games would be to our culture. The ownership our players took during the pre-season was a cornerstone to the success in front of us. They also taught me a crucial lesson in team building – giving them ownership and giving up control will make your team more productive.

Everything Matters

As we emphasized the importance of the pre-season it helped us establish our overall approach before practice even started. My players would hear me use the phrase "everything matters," so much they probably got a little sick of it. By establishing how we were going to operate when they were in the gym and no one was watching, we started to create a mentality.

You simply can't accept less than the best effort from your team in anything they do. It doesn't matter if it's the off-season, if it was just a trial run, or it is outside your regular work hours. If we were going to do it, we were going to do it at a championship level. That was the mentality our program would have. Chip Kelly says, "If you accept it, expect it," and that's a great reminder for leaders. Once you allow for a lower standard—anytime, anywhere—expect your team to meet it.

9

You can't ask your team to act a certain way some of the time. How you operate is who you are, and it doesn't matter if it's a random cold call to your office or a meeting with your biggest client. You can't perform at an elite level some of the time. Elite teams are relentlessly consistent.

Learning How to Win

Those games were also where we started learning how to win. Winning is hard, and I'm a strong believer that it is something you have to learn. But in basketball we get that concept wrong. We talk about teams who lose a lot of close games needing to learn how to win, as if the losing is an essential part of it. Then those teams finally get over the hump and we say they learned how to do it.

You don't learn how to win by losing. You learn how to win by winning. By making winning matter in the pre-season and putting something on it that was motivational (not getting up at 7 AM to run), winning became important to our guys. Competitive excellence mattered. And when they were playing pickup games with no one watching, they were learning how to make plays that helped them win games. They were literally learning how to win.

Internal Accountability

There was something else that the pre-season helped us establish with our culture, and I learned it was essential to any effective leadership model: Internal accountability. Accountability for us was a responsibility to the behaviors that uphold our standards. With any of our core values, we tied them to behavior, as you will see throughout this book.

Once you create ownership in your program, your team needs to hold one another accountable. You have to give them the room to do so. On high performing teams the accountability comes from within. They don't wait for the leadership to do it.

I didn't realize it, but our players ownership in the pre-season helped me establish my coaching philosophy. I wanted to give my team the confidence to make plays. My approach was, "I'll give you the freedom to play on the offensive end, but you have to give me the defensive end." The defensive side was hard, and I was going to be very demanding on that end. The offensive side was theirs. I never wanted guys looking over their shoulder worrying about the play they just made. My confidence to coach that way was borne from the ownership our players took in those pickup games. If a loss means you might have to get up and run at 7 AM on Monday to run, you aren't going to make selfish plays that might hurt your team. If you do, you are going to hear about it from one of your teammates.

For example, our ability to determine what were good shots and what were bad shots came from those pickup games. By the time practice started, I didn't have to coach it. In nine years at RIC I never coached good shot or bad shot. I really didn't. The players always took care of it. They were practicing winning basketball in the pre-season. If you were taking bad shots your teammates would let you know.

Now, I'm not saying we didn't take bad shots. We did. But my point is that stuff was always taken care of by the team. They knew when they took bad shots, and the team would always regulate it. I didn't have to say anything. They were used to hearing it from each other and figuring it out on their own, because of the competitive nature of the pre-season. What was created was a level of internal accountability within our team, from player to player. The guys learned to live up to their own standards and answer to one another before they ever heard from me. That translated directly to our practices on October 15th.

What your people do when they are on their own will not only make them better, it will make you better. Pay attention to it. You don't have to be in control all of the time. Give up control and you'll actually get more out of your team.

There's no doubt the way our guys approached the pre-season made me a better coach. They allowed me to coach the way I wanted to because they took ownership and held each other accountable. The players were already figuring out their issues on the court before they got to practice, and when practice started the accountability was expected.

Find a way within your structure to make your team responsible to one another. If they are accountable to you, you can be good. If they are accountable to each other, you can be great. Internal accountability is a huge part of high achieving organizations.

Attracting Talent

Another important advantage related to those pickup games was in recruiting. Almost every time a recruit came on campus, he'd play with our players. I'll always believe in any basketball program the pickup games are an accurate reflection of who you are, and they are important to recruiting. High achievers are attracted to elite organizations. They can feel the difference. When we had recruits on campus and they played with our guys, they almost always wanted to be a part of it.

Attracting talent is essential to any successful organization. But you don't do it through a flashy sales pitch or a dynamic video presentation. You attract talent by showing them an environment where elite talent and great competitors can thrive. Your recruiting approach isn't the best way for you to attract people to your organization. What your team does every day has a much bigger impact.

Direct Truth Telling

The preseason also allowed me to have conversations with my team that highlighted the importance of being a direct truth teller. I don't know of any highly successful organization without a high level of trust. You have to create an environment where hearing the truth is a comfort zone.

As an assistant coach, I never liked the idea of being careful around our players with regards to recruiting. When we had kids on campus, I didn't worry about the players who played their position, who might be concerned that we were recruiting someone to replace them. Or about the recruit seeing that we had too many guys who played his position. Everybody knew it was our job to recruit the best players, so why were we trying to hide it?

Before we started practice, we had a meeting about recruiting. I told the players we needed them to help recruit more talent to the program. "I am recruiting over you from day one," I told them. "Any coach who ever tells you otherwise is lying. It's my job to get the best talent I can for this program. It's your job to make sure you don't lose your job, so keep getting better. But we are always going to recruit the best players we can get." I think the guys were stunned at first, but when the dust settled, they appreciated the honesty. I was never going to make a recruit more important than any of them. But I was going to tell them the truth. Honest conversation and a strong sense of trust would be crucial for our program.

Telling the truth directly and consistently is important, and it doesn't' happen as often as it should, because it is also hard. Sometimes it requires a difficult conversation and involves disagreement. But handling direct communication isn't nearly as hard as overcoming a lack of trust. Your team will always appreciate hearing the truth, no matter how hard it may be to deal with. People who don't appreciate the truth are very hard to win with. Work on communicating directly and sincerely within your team, and the strength of your trust will grow.

TWO

MENTALITY AND IDENTITY

As an assistant coach, I learned there are two kinds of head coaches in practice – those who clap when the ball goes in, and those who get pissed off when the ball goes in. Most coaches I've seen clap when the ball goes in – they are happy when their team scores. Tim Welsh, who I worked for at Providence College, was one of those guys, more of an offensive minded coach who liked to see the ball go in the basket. As his assistant, I became the defensive guy. That's where I was needed the most. When the offense scored and other people were clapping, I was talking to the defense about where they broke down. I was learning and growing as a coach, and coaching the defense became part of my identity. I didn't want to see the ball going in the hoop.

By the time I became a head coach I knew that was my identity. When you take over as the leader, it's important to know exactly who you are. What are your nonnegotiables—the stuff that is worth fighting for? Once you know that, you can start to work on the organization. Defensive effort was my first nonnegotiable.

Look at the big picture and start with the endgame in mind. What are we going to be about as an organization? What is our identity going to be? You have to know what you expect it to look like. You

15

can then work back from that vision and build the steps to getting there. But it starts with implanting your identity within the organization. The vision that comes from your identity is what drives the steps to building your culture.

Separating Your Team

When I took over at RIC, I knew what my approach was going to be from a basketball perspective—we were going to win with defense. Everyone wants to score. When the players work out or play in the off-season, they aren't doing defensive slides and taking charges. They are shooting the ball. They are working on offensive skills. I felt strongly, and still do, that the defensive side of the ball was where teams could really separate themselves. It just isn't an area where most players—or coaches—are naturally that invested. If you can get your team fully invested on the defensive side of the ball, you can distance yourself from the competition.

It was also the side of the ball I felt was easier to control. Great offensive teams have talent, skill, and ability. Great defensive teams can rely more on approach, effort, and toughness. You can run great offense and get the exact shot you want and just have a bad night shooting, and you really can't control that. But if you are committed defensively, you can be good every night. It allows you to get more out of average talent if you have kids who are tough and wiling to compete. And it creates consistency, because defensively you are relying on things that are almost all within your control. I wanted our defense to be a constant when I became a head coach. I wasn't aware of it yet, but our defense would really separate us from our competition.

Your organizational identity has to fit your vision, and you have to attract personnel that fit that identity. A great challenge is to find an identity that separates you from the competition. Can you find something that is a little bit different, that the other companies in your field aren't paying much attention to? That is the most powerful identity—the kind that separates you. If you can't find an identity that separates you, you'll have to be better than your competition at everything they are already doing. While that is certainly possible, it might be more challenging than finding differentiating characteristics. Get comfortable with an identity that is a little different and your team will do the same.

Team Mentality - Finding Change Areas

Right before practice started, I wanted to focus on our mentality. I took over a team with no history of success that had a reputation within the league for struggling to win important games. I wanted things to be different. This is common practice when taking over a new organization, especially one that isn't used to success. But if you want things to be different, you have to make sure your team can see, hear, and feel a difference. You have to show them tangible change. My goal was to find specific change areas, so that everything our guys saw and did felt different.

The first change area would be our defense. I researched the league (the Little East Conference) and analyzed the statistics of the best teams from the previous season. Luckily for my approach, it was a high octane, offense-first league. Half the teams averaged over 80 points per game, or close to it. It was clearly a league where the best teams outscored everyone else. In watching some film, the defense was indifferent, to say the least. It was brutal. Nobody seemed to care if the other team scored, they were just happy to have the ball back.

My identity fit perfectly with a change in approach. I knew I wanted us to have a defensive mentality. The fact that mentality would make us different than most teams in the league made it a perfect fit. We were going to guard, and we were going to be different than everyone else.

Finding specific change areas can really help your leadership approach when establishing a new culture. Analyze the organization first and figure out why they haven't been successful. Know the facts.

Then figure out the change areas and start to work on how you can actually make it happen. When your personnel can see and feel actual change – and not just hear it from you – they will start to believe in your leadership. You've taken the first step towards establishing your culture.

Creating Buy-In

In that pre-practice team meeting I asked our guys if they thought we were good enough to win the league. It's a great place to start for two reasons – one is I want them to say it and own it. The second is no team with anyone who is half a competitor on it is going to say no, they don't think they can win the league. You won't get much debate. I wanted them to set a high standard for themselves, and that standard was to win the league. And I wanted to hear them say it to me to enhance their level of buy-in.

Once they told me they thought we were good enough to win the league, the next question was how? What are you guys willing to do differently? We were talking about something that had never been done before – RIC had never won the league. They had never even played in the league championship game. I wanted to make it clear that change had to take place. What we have been doing hasn't been good enough to reach that standard, so we have to talk about what we'll do differently.

By establishing a new standard and getting them to own it, we could take steps towards building an approach. Again, asking questions is so important. I wanted them to say it, to be able to own it. When you work toward your goals as an organization, get your people to talk about it. Then you can discuss the steps you have to take together to get there—and make sure they realize it's not going to be easy.

The players set the standard—win the league—and then I got them to tell me how we were going to get there. It was becoming theirs, and they didn't even know it. The way we were going to be different on the court was by playing defense. But I wanted to make sure they had all of the tangible information in front of them so they could see where we had to change. In establishing a new culture, this is very important. The more specifics they can see the more impact you can have.

I put the offensive numbers of every team in the league up on the board in that team meeting. I think Western Connecticut had led the league in scoring the previous year at like 87 points per game. RIC had finished somewhere in the middle of the pack. I did the math on how many possessions would have to change for us to beat the teams above us in the standings, and it was roughly four possessions. If we could get four more stops per game against the top four teams in the league, we'd be in first place. I asked them if that was possible. Can we win four more possessions? We talked about going to West Conn or Keene State and getting two more stops per half. That doesn't sound like a lot to ask. But that was the difference between leading the league in scoring with our offensive numbers and finishing in the middle of the pack.

I used their own words as the fuel. That's why it's so important to collaborate with your team and get them to tell you what they want, what they believe. *You guys told me we are good enough to win the league. You've seen the evidence, where it's going to take about four more stops per game to get the job done. You said it really matters to you. So now I'm going to push you to get there. I'm going to demand more out of you on the defensive end then you have ever given. And we are going to commit to being in the best possible shape we can be in to be great defensively. You guys told me you were capable, and you told me it was important to you. Now you have to buy-in and trust me to get us there.*

My general philosophy as a head coach started to take shape that day. I had a pretty good idea what my approach would be when I got a head coaching job, but seeing it on the board and talking it out ignited me. I wanted a team that was tough and committed on the defensive end, but that played with freedom and confidence on offense. I knew the defensive end could separate us, especially in the Little East Conference.

Be specific about your own identity as a leader, and intentional about the identity of your organization. Identify areas of change that can help you, and where your team will really see and feel a difference. Show them the facts. Ask them a lot of questions to get them to take ownership, and to tell you what they are willing to do.

Leadership isn't getting your team to buy-in to what you are selling. Leadership is getting them to buy-in to something they believe. Creating that dynamic is a difference maker. Our identity started to form that day, as did our belief.

Control

When I was an assistant at Providence, I was lucky to spend some time with Joe Mullaney, the legendary Friars coach who also went on to coach the Los Angeles Lakers. Coach Mullaney had a huge impact on the game, given credit for being the first coach to play a matchup zone. He used to come by the office in our first couple of years at PC and tell stories and talk hoops for hours. How lucky was I as a 26-year-old assistant coach to have those conversations with a coaching legend? One thing Coach Mullaney always said was, "The hardest part about leadership is giving the players control. You have to learn to let them go."

To get the most out of your personnel, you have to let them be themselves. I firmly believe that. Too often we think leadership is about having control, when in fact great leadership is learning how to give up control. The more control you give to your team, the more you are going to get out of them. The goal is to get control to the people who are making the decisions in the heat of the action. Whether it's a sales team, a law firm, or a restaurant, the people making key decisions have to be empowered to do so.

I promised our guys, "I'll give you the offensive end, if you commit to me on the defensive end." We had already talked about the defense, and on offense we adopted an approach that the military uses preparing troops for battle. The saying is "in command, without control." We would train our guys to play a certain way – unselfish, with freedom and confidence – and then when the games started, trust them to play that way. When I told the guys that I was giving them the offensive end if they'd give me the defensive end, their eyes lit up. And I knew I had to give them something. I didn't want them walking out of that meeting thinking practice was going to be brutal or the game wouldn't be a lot of fun because we were going to do defensive slides all day long. I needed to create buy-in, and by talking about the freedom they would have on offense I helped create that buy-in on defense.

How are you giving your team the control they need to succeed? It might be uncomfortable at first, because it doesn't feel natural. But it's the best way to get the most out of them. The goal is to create leaders on your team, not followers. Empowering your team to take control is essential. Don't demand control as a leader. Learn to distribute it.

Defining Your System

I didn't know it at the time, but the most important basketball element I brought to the program as a new head coach had to do with definition. It was a defined defensive system. It is the first piece of basketball advice I give to anyone who is a new head coach. Figure out exactly who you want to be defensively and define it specifically for your players. I don't care what system it is—play zone, man-to-man, press, pack line—whatever you want. But define it clearly for your guys so they know exactly what to expect.

Clear definition is essential to strong leadership. What can you do to separate yourself the most from your competition (be great defensively), and how are you going to make it happen (define it). The crucial elements of your organizational approach need to be clear and defined, and this is somewhere basketball coaches often get lost. Our personnel changes year to year, and our opponent changes game to game. Throw in the advances made in scouting at the college level and it's very easy to constantly change. Your approach becomes less and less defined as you continue to tweak it, making it harder for your team to understand and buy-in. Consistency is something your people can count on and it gives them confidence. You can provide it for them. Great organizations know what to expect.

Our defensive system was one that I learned as an assistant at the University of San Diego when I was there for one year, and it came from a great high school coach in Arizona named Royce Youree. I added some stuff that I liked over the years working in the Big East, and it fit the athletic personnel we had at RIC very well. Certainly, the right fit matters. The defensive system I brought to the program fit best with athletic personnel, and at RIC I took over the most athletic team in the league. But the most important thing was we had a system. It was set, it was defined, and other than minor adjustments it didn't change. Our players can still, to this day, look at any possession of any basketball game and know where the breakdown was and who was supposed to help. There was no gray area. Defining our system was the most important basketball decision I made as a first year head coach. I didn't realize it was such an important leadership decision as well.

Once you have established your identity as an organization and what is important to you, figure out how to define it for your team. Be specific. If your people don't have a clear grasp on what you are doing and what is expected, they can't completely buy-in. You don't want your team thinking about what's important, they have to know. Eliminate any doubt.

Many leaders make this mistake, assuming that a lack of buy-in is based on the approach of their personnel. Very often that lack of buy-in is due to a leadership mistake – the lack of clear definition. If they are confused about what's expected of them, how are they supposed to buy-in? This requires great preparation and commitment from you as the leader. Figure out what is important to you and deliver it in a clear, concise manner. You can always make adjustments. But to get complete buy-in from your organization, the way you define things for them is crucial.

Confidence

Over time there were so many benefits to having a defined defensive system. It allowed us to hold our guys accountable with consistency. Once they understood the system, they knew exactly who was supposed to be where and how they needed to move together. Their responsibilities were clear. A major obstacle for many teams is indecision, and a defined system takes care of that. When you give your team options, they will usually take the path of least resistance. Eliminate that with definition.

A defined system can also do great things for your team's confidence. I never really thought about confidence on the defensive side of the ball until I became a head coach, and I don't think most coaches do. But once our guys understood the system and started to believe in it, the mentality changed. We walked into every gym expecting to win because our guys knew we were going to be tough to score on. That brought with it a lot of confidence.

It also helped that guys knew exactly when they screwed up. There was no confusion. We made plenty of mistakes like every team. But we knew how to fix them, and we could always identify the breakdown. When we got comfortable with it, there was no indecision. One of my favorite sayings was, "It's more important to be decisive than to be right." It turned out to be a great way to build confidence. We weren't evaluated based on the result. It was always based on executing our system. Sometimes the other team scored. We weren't going to shut any teams out. But there was no indecision between two guys not knowing who was supposed to be where, and that really made us a confident team.

Our system stayed the same, regardless of who we played or specific personnel. In nine years at RIC we never once changed something we did defensively based on a scouting report. In today's game, with all the film available and the emphasis on scouting, that may seem a little odd, but I really believe in it. Of course, we scouted other teams and we knew player tendencies, but we never changed our core principles. Sticking with our defensive system did more for our confidence than I ever could have imagined.

Confidence is often overlooked and under coached. Most leaders want a confident team, yet we don't necessarily coach it. Think about the confidence of your organization and your personnel when defining your process. If confidence is important to you—and it should be—than define your process for everyone in the organization. Make sure they know what is expected of them without hesitation. They will be decisive even if they aren't always right. That confidence is energy for a high achieving organization.

What separated us during our nine-year dynasty at Rhode Island College was being the best defensive team in the league. We had a lot of talent on both ends of the floor, without question, but it was our commitment on the defensive end that made us different. It was an approach that helped set the tone for our change in culture when I took over. And more importantly, like I had hoped, it gave us a chance to win every night. Great defense travels. Great defense overcomes injury. Great defense allows role players to make an impact. And the confidence it helped build in what we were doing was immeasurable. The single most important factor in our sustained success – and our eight straight NCAA bids – was the fact that we were consistently the best defensive team in the league.

When we left that meeting room before practice started, our guys had the facts in front of them. They saw how a change in commitment on the defensive end of the floor could make a big difference. They didn't know anything about how we were going to play yet or what it would look like, but it was the first step in believing in the hard stuff it takes to win championships consistently. They had told me we were good enough to win the league, and I gave them a tangible path to get there.

We went out and had t-shirts made up that said "Win the League" on the back. My creativity for t-shirt slogans clearly needed some work, but hey, at least the message was clear.

Confirmation Bias

NCAA division III rules don't allow you to have any practices or workouts with your team before October 15th. Not even tryouts. There were always 5-10 guys interested in going out for the team that hadn't been with the team the year before. They would hang out with the players, play pickup with them, and show up when they were lifting, but you really didn't know your full team until two or three days after practice started.

That fall we had 11 guys returning, with another 10-12 interested in making the team. We couldn't pick the team until practice started, and practice couldn't start until October 15th, so the first two or three days of practice were pretty hectic. We had to do more than just play tryout games and watch them play, but running a practice with 20-25 guys, about eight of whom you know have no chance of being on the team, isn't easy. But those tryouts that year taught me a great lesson in evaluating talent.

Cameron Stewart went to Rogers High School in Newport, Rhode Island and enrolled at RIC in 2004 as a regular student. He wasn't recruited to play basketball. He played intramurals as a freshman (the year before I got the RIC job) and a bunch of the basketball players used to referee intramural games (as the head coach at RIC, you also ran intramurals). A few of the players got to know Cam through refereeing his intramural games and thought he was pretty good, so they convinced him to go out for the team. When I arrived at RIC in the fall of 2005, he was one of the 10-12 or so guys that was working out in the pre-season with the players, trying to make the team.

Needless to say, having just taken over my first head job a month earlier, with most of the team returning from the year before, my priority wasn't sorting out the walk-ons. We had them with us in practice for a couple of days and then we were ready to move forward. We sat in the hallway just outside the gym after our second practice—it was pretty late, because at that time of year we went after volleyball and after women's basketball. It was like 10:30 at night and I grabbed my assistants to figure out what we were going to do with the walk-ons.

Cam was a skinny, 6-1 kid who looked like every intramural player playing in college. Nothing stood out about him physically. But I remember something stood out to me about the way he played – the game just came naturally to him. He didn't do anything spectacular, but he just had a comfort zone with the game that I noticed. Nothing was ever forced. He was the topic of conversation in that hallway when we were figuring out who to cut. And still, I thought we were talking about like our 13th best player anyway. We had a returning core that was very good. But I remember saying to my assistants after we talked about it, "I don't think we can cut Cam Stewart." A few of our players had asked about him as well, wanting to know if we were going to take him. They wanted me to know how good they thought he was. But he was definitely on the chopping block. We decided to keep him that night, figuring he'd be a good teammate and nice walk-on to have.

Cam Stewart led the league in three-point field goal percentage as a freshman, scored almost 1,000 points in his career and helped lead us to three straight NCAA Tournaments. He was a crucial part of our championship culture. And he wasn't just a nice walk-on who overachieved, and a skinny kid who could make shots. He was a playmaker. A straight baller. It took me a little while to realize he was the guy we wanted with the ball in his hands when the game was on the line. He just always made the right play (in fact, he single handedly beat Holy Cross for one of our two D1 wins in an exhibition game, scoring our final six points down the stretch). He was a huge part of the success we built, and after two days of practice I was sitting in a hallway at 10:30 at night deciding whether or not he would even make the team.

How much time do you invest in evaluating talent? In college basketball it is obviously essential. I think about Cam Stewart a lot when I'm evaluating. First of all, he taught me the value of having guys on your team who aren't "good enough" (I'll explain more on that later). But he also taught me not to judge a book by its cover when evaluating, and to avoid confirmation bias. Cam was a skinny, non-descript kid that was underestimated his entire career, and made people pay because of it. Even the teams who knew he was a good player thought he was just a shooter, because that's what he looked like. We had a team full of great playmakers throughout my nine years at RIC, but Cam was probably the guy I most wanted to have the ball late in a close game. He just made plays.

It is so easy to see what you expect—or what you want to see—when you are evaluating personnel. It's natural to confirm what you expect – confirmation bias. You start with an idea about what you are going to see, and you focus on the actions that confirm what is in your head. Cam Stewart looked like a smart walk-on who could make an open shot and might be able to help us in practice when he went out for the team. And that's what I expected to see. But, luckily, I took him and gave him a chance, because he ended up being one of the best playmakers I would ever coach.

Self-Awareness

Cam Stewart taught me to clear my mind and make sure I saw things through an unbiased lens. He's one of the greatest players I've ever coached, and he went to RIC to play intramurals. I gave him two days of tryouts and then almost cut him. I'll never take a walk-on or tryout situation for granted again. And I'll always make sure to look for things I don't expect to see.

Self-awareness is a critical component of leadership. Knowing your strengths and weaknesses and how your experiences might impact your ability to evaluate is crucial. I know in my business it is easy to put people in a box. Stereotypes are prevalent and it's so easy to see what you expected to see.

As the leader, collect diverse opinions and clear your mind to look for things you might not expect. Make sure you are aware of it. Challenge your staff to disagree with you, to give you a different approach. Your mind can play tricks on you, and it almost cost me one of the best players I've ever coached.

THREE

THE LESSONS OF LEADERSHIP

OCTOBER 15, 2005 (FIRST DAY OF PRACTICE)

Getting my first head coaching job at a division III state school was a great training ground as a basketball coach. There wasn't a lot of money or a lot of bells and whistles. I learned to be low maintenance, not to ask for anything, and to make the most out of what we had.

The first day of practice is always big, but especially as a first year head coach. You finally get a chance to run your own practice with your own team. Everything you've thought about as an assistant gets put into action. You are the leader. You know you have to set the right tone. It's an exciting day. I was ready to go.

Win Anyway

Our first practice my first year at RIC wasn't even held in our gym. There was an Admissions Open House on campus that day, and they were using the Murray Center, where we practiced and played. My first practice as a head coach would be in the student recreation center. Curtains down, students running around the track, nothing private about it. And on top of that, it was pouring rain outside. And guess what kind of roof they have at the student recreation center at a D3 state school? Well, not exactly a great one. As we prepared for practice there were three different leaks draining water from the roof onto our practice floor. I stood in the hallway 15 minutes before practice as the supervisor of the recreation center explained to me how he would use half-court drills when this happened to him as a high school coach. Great, my first day of practice and we are going to play half-court.

Somehow, we got through that one—our assistants chasing down towels and wiping the floor constantly—and we were able to get into the Murray Center the next day. We were fortunate that RIC really did have great facilities, and the Murray Center was terrific. What I didn't realize was that on the other side of the bleachers was the gymnastics pit, and the gymnastics team practiced at the same time as we did so we could share a trainer. As we gathered at half-court for our first practice in the Murray Center, underneath one of the baskets were six gymnasts lining up in their leotards. They were practicing the vault, and the run-up to the vault extended all the way underneath the far hoop. So much for starting with an intense shell drill. I realized pretty quickly I wasn't in the Big East anymore. I also got to catch up on a lot of pop music from the 80s that was blasted over the bleachers from the gymnastics pit.

Truth is, what I also realized was how easily we can get distracted by things that don't really matter. We all want a quiet gym and everyone's undivided attention for every minute of practice. Head coaches are notorious control freaks who don't want to hear doors opening, music playing, or people walking in and out of practice. And the temperature had better be just right. The reality is this doesn't make sense. We want total control of our practice environment, but we don't ever play games under those conditions. Why are we so concerned with those conditions when we are having practice? One of the best things you can do when you take over as a leader is get over yourself.

At RIC we usually had gymnastics in the gym, and we sometimes had wrestling in the gym. We always practiced either right after volleyball or right before women's basketball—there were always teams coming in and out. We also shared the building with physical education, so professors and students were walking through. At first, I was a little annoyed because I wanted total control. But being forced to deal with some of that made me realize something—I'd rather not have a controlled environment for practice. If I can't get my guys to focus because the volleyball team is in the gym stretching or somebody opens one of the doors, how are we going to win in a tough gym on the road? All that stuff helped us become a low maintenance program because we had no other choice. As the leader, I realized I needed to pour my energy into what really mattered, and not worry about minor distractions. It would have been easy to make a big deal out of that stuff, when in fact the minor distractions actually made us mentally tougher.

(I've always found it hysterical when I am watching somebody else's practice and the clock is running down. You see managers sprinting over to the clock to stop it before the horn goes off as if they are worried a bomb is about to explode. Coaches can take themselves way too seriously. It's basketball, people. Sometimes the buzzer goes off. We'll all survive. I'm sure of it).

The challenges we faced at RIC helped shape our culture and made me a better leader. The circumstances forced us to develop a low maintenance, no excuses mentality, and that became part of our ethos. We learned to focus on what really mattered, because we had no choice. Any team can do the same. Embrace the challenges you face and turn them into a level of mental toughness that can drive you.

The phrase we started to adopt was "Win anyway." That was our approach. There's a leak in the roof? Win anyway. We have to share the gym? Win anyway. The bus showed up late? Win anyway. "Win anyway" came to represent the mental toughness in our program. It was our way of saying no excuses, that we were prepared to handle anything. It was an approach that came to define us, that both fit perfectly and was borne out of the challenges we faced at a division III state school.

I also learned that developing our team culture was a lot easier if it fit with the culture of our school. Rhode Island College is a state school in a capital city, and it is a practical, inexpensive education that attracted a lot of first generation college students. The school is blue collar, tough and low maintenance by nature. The culture we developed as a program fit naturally.

The environment you are in is going to attract a certain type of person. You can swim against the tide if you want and try and make your business or program different, but if you do so you are only adding to the challenge. Be realistic about the culture of your institution and the type of players or employees you will be able to attract. It's not always easy, finding the right fit with the level of talent you need to succeed. I understand that. But your culture will grow stronger as you add personnel who fit in, feel comfortable and are willing to fight for it.

Trust – My First Big Mistake

As we got into the routine of practice every day, I made my first big mistake as a head coach. But as is the case with most leadership mistakes, I didn't realize it until after the fact. If you could see it coming, well, you'd avoid the mistake. This one would take me a while to figure out.

The foundation of our program was how hard we competed every day. That was made very clear to everyone from day one, that our compete level was within our control and that was how we would be evaluated. We were going to be completely process based—focusing on the way we approached practice and not worrying about results. On October 15th, that's where we started. And that's the culture we would eventually establish. But the mistake I made—and I didn't realize it at the time—was that I didn't really earn my team's trust. We had a talented team with most of the players back, and I knew we had a chance to be good. They had won 20 games the year before but had lost in the league semi-finals to end their season. This was a good team that just needed to get to the next level by winning the big games. I didn't realize it at the time but looking back it's pretty clear. I took over the best team in the league my first year.

I knew we were pretty good, and I knew we were a veteran team. I wanted to make sure everyone was comfortable. My mistake was trying to fit in with the guys, rather than earning their trust and putting my own personality on the program. Anytime you take over a new organization—whether the organization is successful or not—things are going to be different. The culture is going to change. The voice of the new leader is different, as is the emphasis. How the players respond will also be different. We had new leadership, and for better or worse, things were going to change. It was inevitable, and I didn't understand that.

You have to be yourself. That was another mistake I made, because I was trying to fit in. There may be some bumps in the road, and that is to be expected. You have to be able to handle that. But I was treading lightly with my new team, even though I didn't think I was. I wanted them to like me (a natural feeling to have, whether you admit it or not) when it was more important that they trust me and respect me. I was trying to fit in and keep things comfortable without realizing it.

When you take over, establishing who you are and what matters to you is important. This doesn't mean you have to be a hard-ass or bring a negative tone every day. But you have to establish what you are all about. I was telling my team who I was, but I wasn't showing it to them every day. I was trying to fit in, as a coach they would like. I wasn't being myself. Subconsciously, I was being the coach I thought they wanted.

Be intentional about establishing your personality immediately. There may be some resistance, but your team will see you as genuine and you will start to develop the most important piece of currency in high achieving organizations—trust. Without trust, they can like you as much as you want but you aren't going anywhere. To trust you they have to see you as authentic.

I was trying to fit in with my players to make sure I didn't rock the boat, even though that wasn't my plan. I thought our practices were good and our team was competing really hard, but I gradually learned that was not the case. And how could it be? I was using the word compete all of the time, but I wasn't demanding the right compete level out of them or holding them accountable to my standards. I learned that lesson the hard way as we were really inconsistent right from the start. My players liked playing for me, but they didn't trust me. It would take me until January to figure it out.

Embrace Change

It's interesting that I didn't really earn the trust of my team early on from a mental standpoint, because I wasn't afraid to make basketball changes. Kamari Williams was a junior guard from Springfield, Massachusetts, and he was one of the best players in the league. He had started as the point guard as a freshmen and sophomore, earning all-rookie and all-league honors in those years. He was a very intelligent player who could run a team as well as score. He was a stocky guard who wasn't lightning quick but was very crafty and an excellent passer. He was considered our best player.

Kinsey Durgin was a junior guard from Bethel, Maine on that first team as well, a lightning quick combo guard who could get up and down and could also shoot. He had the ability to handle the ball, and I thought he could be a great defender. He was also very smart and could make his teammates better. I knew after the first few days of practice that we had a very talented backcourt – a great backbone to be a great team.

I also knew I wanted to make a change. Kamari wasn't in great shape early in the year, and Kinsey was more of what I wanted out of a point guard. He was fast, he could get the ball where he wanted it, and he could keep the other team from getting it where they wanted it. Kamari didn't get the ball up the court quickly and was generally more deliberate. I wanted the ball to move. Based on what I saw, Kinsey was our point guard and Kamari would play off the ball. I was going to switch their positions.

I find it interesting that from a leadership and accountability standpoint with regards to the way we competed, I was timid. But from a basketball perspective, I wasn't afraid to make a change that would alter the dynamic of our lineup. At the time I don't remember thinking it was that big of a deal. Both guys were good, both guys would play, they'd just play different positions.

Making a key change like that early on—especially with your two best players—isn't an easy decision. But I was going with what I saw every day and what I knew fit my style. Looking back, I'm a little surprised but certainly glad I had the conviction to make the change. It would have been easy to keep things status quo given a veteran team that had experienced success the year before. But I was convinced it was the right thing to do, and it turned out I was right. If your gut tells you something needs to change, you probably need to do it, regardless of the level of success you have experienced. And when you are just taking over, the sooner you make the change the better.

I was prepared for the basketball dynamic and confident in what I was doing. But I hadn't thought about the leadership dynamic. I had studied the basketball stuff for years and it came easy to me. The leadership stuff was all brand new.

The Impact of Change
November 2005

While it turned out I made the right decision with Kamari and Kinsey, where I screwed up was not thinking about the impact the change had on my team. And it probably cost me my first loss as a head coach.

Practice continued going pretty well (or so I thought), and we had implemented the style of play I wanted—fast and aggressive. We wanted to attack on both ends of the floor and we had the talent and depth to do it. I thought we had a chance to be very good, and I loved the kids I was coaching. It was mid-November and we were ready for the season to start.

We opened up in Wheaton's tip-off tournament against Mt. Ida, and we beat them pretty easily for my first win as a head coach. The guys felt good about the way we played and the results. The next night we played Wheaton at their place in the championship game, and we came out playing well again. We were up 5-7 points most of the last 10 minutes, and I thought we had a better team. It was a game we should have won.

We had a two-guard who came off the bench on that team from New Haven, Connecticut named Davon Yarbrough who was very talented, tough and no nonsense. He had a chip on his shoulder every time he took the court. My kind of player. Devo was playing very well that night against Wheaton. Down the stretch I had Kinsey and Devo in the backcourt, with Kamari Williams on the bench. Kinsey and Devo had played well together, and I stayed with it.

Late in that game we fell apart. Devo had a couple of costly turnovers, and our team started to panic. We still had a good chance to win but never settled back down. We blew the lead and lost the game. I had spent 24 glorious hours undefeated as a head coach. But that first loss stung. I knew we were the better team and we should have won the game. Somehow, we had coughed it up.

Kyle Smith is a close friend and former college teammate of mine who went on to be the head coach at Columbia, the University of San Francisco and Washington State. Kyle was two years ahead of me at Hamilton, and at the time he was an assistant coach for Randy

Bennett at St. Mary's. He was on the east coast recruiting at a tournament that weekend and had taken a ride to watch us play.

After the game we were going through the plays down the stretch and I explained to him the dynamic with our back court. I was obviously pretty down about the way we lost. Kyle said from watching the game, he thought I was probably right, that Devo and Kinsey belonged out there. But then he said something really interesting. "The problem is, in a game like that, what your players are comfortable with is probably more important. They are used to having Kamari in there with the ball. He's the one that settles things down. That change may be the right one, but you have to think about the impact it has on them."

It was a brilliant point, something I hadn't considered. And an important leadership lesson. Even though I felt good about the change I made, I hadn't thoroughly examined the impact it might have on my team—especially in a close game. To them, Kamari was the quarterback. He played under control, rarely turned the ball over and made his free throws. He was the guy they were used to having the ball late in close games. Without him on the floor, when things got a little hectic, they didn't know how to respond. They were looking for him out there. I had gotten them out of their comfort zone with a decision I made, and I hadn't properly addressed it.

Would we have won that game with Kamari on the floor? My gut tells me, yes. We'll never know the answer. I hadn't thought about how my decision might impact the mentality of my players. I hadn't explained to them what I was thinking or why I was making the move. They just looked up in a close game and saw Kamari on the bench when things were falling apart. And they weren't comfortable with it.

It was a great lesson on the impact of the mental side of the game. It's important for you to make the necessary changes to help your organization. And it takes guts to make those changes. But you also have to make sure your team understands your approach to change.

They have to know why. If they don't, at the first sign of discomfort they will start to question your decision. That's a mistake I made, and the decision cost us our first loss that year.

And it's a decision that would have an impact in the most important game of the season, later that year.

The Message They Receive

Despite that tough loss, I was having a blast coaching my team. I loved the guys we had—talented, tough, and fun to be around. We were deep and athletic, and I thought we were practicing at a high level. I loved being in the gym with them. There was just one problem—we were really inconsistent.

On some nights we looked great. We played hard and together, and we were really sharp. We were a nightmare matchup for most teams in our region. But other nights we didn't bring it. We didn't compete that hard, we were out of sync, and it just didn't seem to matter that much. While I thought we were competing hard in practice every day, obviously something wasn't translating. We were losing to teams who had no business beating us.

I knew what the message was that I was sending—that we were going to be defined by the way we competed every day. I talked about competing all of the time. But it didn't seem like they were getting the message, and that was more important. The message your team receives is what really matters, and it might not be the same message. You are responsible for the message as the leader, and if they don't get it, it's on you.

I didn't know whether I was confusing my team or they just didn't trust me as the messenger. Our schedule was packed in really tight in November and December, and we were playing three games in most weeks. We never got any sort of consistency. As we got into December and the end of the first semester we were finding a way to lose to teams that should never have beaten us. We finished the first semester just a game over .500.

I heard a lot of coach-speak from my friends in the business—it will take time, you have to get your own players in there, but I wasn't buying it. We had a lot of talent and we were losing games we shouldn't lose. I knew something was wrong. The team wasn't responding to what I was saying, and I had to figure that out.

Never Blame Your Team
January 2006

One thing I refused to do was blame the players. This is a critical leadership mistake and I had seen it as an assistant. It's something leaders will do to make themselves more comfortable and avoid the challenge of finding the real problem. Blaming the team is a dangerous game. Once you go down that road, it's hard to ever come back. The connection becomes unbalanced. It's an, "I led well, you performed poorly" approach, a trap that is all too common, and an easy way to lose your team. I refused to go there.

I evaluated my team honestly and I knew I really liked them. I liked the make-up, I liked the talent, I liked the approach. We had tough, hungry kids who were athletic and gifted. I said to my staff "It's not like I want to recruit new players. I'd recruit these guys all over again." We weren't going to blame the players and bring in "our own guys." These were my guys. I was their coach. Something we were doing wasn't working, and there was a disconnect. If you want accountability in your organization, you'd better be willing to hold yourself accountable first and foremost. I had to figure it out.

We came back after Christmas break and continued our uneven play for the first two weeks. We were 8-6 and headed to Western Connecticut for a league game in mid-January, still trying to figure it out. The day we headed to West Conn I finally found the answer. Or more accurately, the answer found me. It would turn out to be one of the most important days of my coaching career.

We had an 11:00 AM practice the day of the game and I walked into the gym at about 10:50. Kinsey Durgin was the only player I saw shooting around. It was odd to me that there wasn't one other player in the gym. I waited about five minutes, and Kinsey was still the only player in the gym. I asked him where everyone else was.

"I don't know. Downstairs I guess." Our locker room was downstairs. The guys were in the building, they just hadn't made it up to the gym yet. Eleven O'clock came and went and Kinsey was still the only player on the court.

About 11:05, a few of the guys started to make their way into the gym. By 11:10, the entire team was in there, shooting around casually, waiting for me to blow the whistle. Nothing seemed out of the ordinary to them. They were just waiting for me to start practice.

Before we began, I asked the team a question. "What time was practice today, fellas?"

"11:00," they all responded quickly, looking at me somewhat perplexed as to why I was even asking the question.

Interesting, I thought. I had my answer.

I knew there was nothing confusing about that message. Practice started at 11:00 AM and they all knew it. There was no mixed message. It just didn't matter to them that much. They didn't really trust me as the messenger. I said it, and they knew it, but it just wasn't that important. They were all in the building, but they would get into the gym when they were ready. Practice starting at 11:00 wasn't that big of a deal.

Of course, it was a big deal. And now the answer was clear to me. The message was not the problem. They didn't trust the messenger.

Discipline

I've never been a big believer in imposing discipline on game day. This is an easy place to dig yourself into a hole. It's easy to make too big of a deal about something on game day and put your team in a bad situation. If you are running a business and you have a huge presentation one day, but someone on your staff screws up, what are you going to do? You are going to get through the presentation, get the job done, and then deal with it. You aren't going to blow the deal.

I look at my team the same way. There are certainly some violations of our standards that add up to being suspended for games but being late for practice isn't one of them. I don't think the offense is any greater because it takes place on game day. If one of our players is late for practice or late for class, there is a penalty. Usually we'll run as a team, and that generally gets the message across. But being late for a game or practice isn't going to get you benched for a game, and I don't think game day should be any different. I want to handle our discipline in a way that will make the point, strengthen our culture, but without unnecessarily hurting our team even more. I think many coaches make a mistake here because of the heightened intensity of game day.

Accountability is important in any organization, but think about the best way to strengthen your culture when you send the message. Whatever your "game day" is, I'm not sure it should be upended by a minor violation. Don't get me wrong, I'm not advocating for being lenient with discipline. If someone needs to be benched, bench them. Just don't overreact to a minor violation of your standards because of when it happened.

When someone was late for a game day practice, I'd usually put my whistle in my jacket pocket for the game without saying anything. I wanted to focus on the game. When the game ended, before our guys left the floor, I'd bring them together and deliver the message about whatever standards we had not lived up to. I'd put them on the baseline, and we'd start running sprints. That usually got the message across pretty clearly. It was a little embarrassing for the kids in front of their parents, but it also sent a strong message about the importance of our culture. I thought it was better than impacting our ability to win a game over a minor violation, which I felt could impact my credibility as a leader.

Of course, on this day I knew we had a significant problem. I also knew we weren't going to address it properly right then and there. I had to let it go. We had our game day practice and went to West Conn to try and win. I set aside the fact that guys were late until after the game. Adding to the issues, two of our players who were injured didn't bring the proper attire to wear. We didn't allow our guys to wear sweat suits on the bench, and everyone knew that. Injured players had to wear a collared shirt, and slacks. The two guys who wore sweats sat in the stands to watch the game.

We lost that night to fall to 8-7. The result had nothing to do with our game day practice or guys being late. It was just more inconsistent play from an inconsistent team. I didn't say anything about the guys being late for practice that day. We didn't run after the game because we were on the road and we had to get home. This was bigger than that. My guess was the guys didn't even think twice about it after the game.

But now I knew things needed to change, and I knew why. I thought my team was bought in to what we were doing, but the truth is they weren't. And it was my fault. As the leader, they didn't trust me, that what I was telling them really mattered. Because I was being inconsistent. I was talking to them about competing every day, but I wasn't demanding it out of them. They didn't really believe in me because I hadn't been following through with the message.

Get the Message

The following day we had what our players still refer to as the "Get the Message" practice.

When the guys came up from the locker room the day after the West Conn game there were no balls in the gym. They noticed that was a little different and they just stood around for a little bit until the clock ran out and I was ready to start. When the horn went off, I told everyone to get on the baseline. But things were different this time. They had to be. When I said on the baseline, I meant literally everyone had to be standing on the baseline. When I blew the whistle and I was talking, everyone had to be looking at me. Everyone's jerseys had to be tucked in at all times. I literally walked up and down the baseline and made sure every one of them was standing on it. If the message was on the baseline, it meant exactly that – stand on the baseline. I had a much sharper and louder tone in my voice, and the message was extremely clear and direct. They knew things were different.

I explained to them that it was clear that they didn't trust me, and it was my fault. I may have confused them at some point with my message and I apologized for that, but the practice time was very clear. I asked them what time practice was yesterday and they all agreed it was 11:00. They knew what time they were supposed to be in the gym, the reality was it just didn't matter to them. It was clear to me that they felt comfortable disregarding my message.

That was going to change. From that day forward in our program things were going to be different. It was never going to be okay to disregard the message.

We never took the basketballs out for practice that day. We started running suicides in 30 seconds. We had to run one each for the 12 guys that were late for practice, and then one each for the two guys who went on the road without the proper gear to wear on the bench. 14 suicides, all in 30 seconds. When we stopped making our times, we just added more suicides to the total. Let's just say we ran a lot. All the time while they were running, I made the same point, very clearly. As I gave them instructions on running, I continued to ask them if the message was clear. It would never again be acceptable to disregard the message in our program.

I knew going into that day things had to change. I also knew that it had to start with something significant. To affect real change, you have to send a very strong message. And you have to follow through on it. That's why I was adamant, from that day forward, about guys literally standing on the baseline when they were told "on the line." There would be no ambiguity with our message. I also knew things had to look and feel different. I took a military-like tone in practice to get the point across. I had accepted the wrong behavior for too long, and our guys needed to leave that day knowing that when they showed up for practice moving forward, things were going to be different. My message, my tone, my approach—everything said things were going to change. And I had to follow through on it.

I also had to apologize. I was responsible for the culture of the program and I hadn't been consistent with the message. I was letting them slide, and they were taking advantage of it. I had been letting them down, and I told them that. It all started with me.

A New Voice

As the leader everything is your responsibility, good or bad – especially the bad. You have to accept that. The approach of our team was my fault, and I realized that. I came in as a first year head coach with a veteran team that had a lot of talent, and I failed to understand that things had to change. Not that we needed to do things differently altogether, but just that things were naturally going to be different, and I had to make sure they bought into that. As a new head coach, the emphasis was going to change. Halfway through my first year as a head coach I started to learn that.

I thought my guys trusted me without ever really earning their trust. They weren't going through the motions, but they were giving me just enough. I wasn't demanding more. I wanted to fit in, and I wanted them to like me. That made me comfortable as a new head coach, but it didn't earn their respect. I wasn't pushing them and holding them accountable to the standards we had established. Respect and trust are essential to any leadership relationship. I hadn't challenged them the way I needed to, and I wasn't getting the most out of them. I hadn't earned their trust. It took me three months of the season and seven losses to figure it out.

The Leadership Model

I was confident after that practice that our players understood. They recognized things were going to be different and that adhering to the message was required. I knew I had to follow up with a consistent approach every day.

I knew that to make sure the point resonated I would need help. I didn't want a dictatorship, and we had started making progress with our players taking ownership. While the strict, intense approach was necessary to get the message across, it wasn't, by itself, the most effective way for me to get the most out of the team. With our change in approach after that Western Connecticut game, it was the perfect time to get more buy-in from my players.

I thought we had pretty good leadership on our team with KP as our only senior. Kinsey Durgin had stepped up as a leader as well. But obviously it could improve given our inconsistent approach. I knew I wanted to put the responsibility for change on our players, so I started to really think about our leadership model.

A standard leadership model works from the top down, with a few leading the many and sending the message as to how the team will operate. While I came up on teams under this model, I was never certain it was the most effective. On teams I was a part of with plenty of players who could contribute in different ways, many weren't comfortable doing so because they didn't hold the right status with the group.

As I grew as a leader and gained more experience, I realized many of my players felt the constraints of the traditional leadership model. I had younger players who were talented and had great leadership qualities but didn't feel comfortable speaking up because it wasn't their team. They felt they had to take a backseat to the veterans and wait their turn. I also had older players who felt they were supposed to speak up because of their status on the team, who weren't delivering the right message. The traditional leadership model could certainly hinder the growth of a team.

Jack Clark, the great rugby coach at Cal, introduced me to a leadership approach when he came and spoke to the coaches at Providence College, and it resonated with me. The idea is that leadership is a skill, and not a rank. It has nothing to do with status, age or talent. Leadership is about making your teammates better, and everyone can do it. It's not something that is just for the captains or the veteran players. It is a skill that can be developed by everyone.

At 8-7 and playing well below our ability, I didn't have a lot to risk. We weren't having a great year, and I was convinced significant change was necessary, so we changed the leadership model. We started by defining leadership for our program. We defined it as "making the people around you better," and we were requiring it out of everybody. You may lead in a different way than your teammates, and you had to find an approach that fit your personality, but leadership was a requirement. It wasn't just the loud guy who spoke up in the locker room to get guys going. It could be showing up 15 minutes early for practice to get some extra shots up. Or making sure your teammates are on time for class. Make the people around you better. Everyone can do it.

Our guys were excited about the new approach. They all felt they could contribute more. With our "Get the Message" practice and our new leadership model we created more room for ownership and buy-in. I really do believe the traditional top-down leadership model limits your team more than it helps. Create a definition of leadership that fits your personality and aligns with your goals and make it simple and attainable for everyone. Get your leadership from the middle of your team, rather than from the top down, and you'll get the most out of everyone.

Captains

Moving forward with this leadership approach, I had to change the way we approached our captains. Traditional captains are part of an outdated leadership model.

I bet I can tell you who the captains are on most teams. They are older players, better players, and louder players. Most organizations are led by experienced people who are good at what they do, and also are not afraid to speak up. As I addressed our leadership model, I had to ask myself the question – does being older, better, and louder make you a great leader? My answer to that is, no. This is an area where I think many of us get leadership wrong.

The best leader who has ever played for me was Antone Gray, a point guard who came to RIC as a freshman in 2007, the year after we went to the Elite Eight. Antone was also the smartest player I'd ever coached. He just had an incredible feel for the people around him and tremendous basketball instincts. When he had a basketball in his hands he glowed, and everyone on the court responded to his energy.

Early on in his first year, we were struggling with a very talented group that was also very young. I had a conversation with Antone, and he told me he wasn't comfortable speaking up in practice because he was just a freshman and he didn't feel like it was "his team." I had gone away from the traditional leadership model, but that's the moment that really woke me up. Here was a natural leader who was my starting point guard, the guy with the ball in his hands in crunch time, and he wasn't comfortable leading when that was exactly what we needed. I was failing the team with an environment that didn't allow for everyone to lead.

At that point, I changed the way we talked about captains. We had to have captains, as someone is required to meet with the officials before the game. From then on, our captains had technical responsibilities only—to meet with the officials, ask them questions when appropriate, handle media requests, and so forth. But the leadership was not the responsibility of the captains. It was the responsibility of everyone. If you are expecting more leadership out of your captains, by definition you are expecting less out of everyone else. That didn't work for me. If you only rely on a chosen few to lead your organization, you are likely suppressing the ability of others who can make you better. With a model that is accessible to all—such as making the people around you better—you can get leadership out of everyone on your team, while increasing the chances of getting the most out of their ability.

Leadership is a skill. Captain is a rank. I recognize that being a captain is an important position and means a lot to the team. But it doesn't mean I expect more leadership out of them than anyone else. A model that empowers everyone on your team to lead, in their own way, can be transformational for your organization.

FOUR

COACHING THE MENTAL GAME

JANUARY 2006

One of the most important things I did after that West Conn game was take ownership of our shortcomings. Leadership is pretty simple in this regard. If you want accountability from your players, hold yourself accountable and be transparent about it. If you want ownership from them, take owner-ship yourself. I was responsible for the tone that was set every day at practice, and it was now obvious our guys were too comfortable. It was my fault. I've always told my coaches "They'll walk if you let them." If you don't demand that the players run from drill to drill, they are going to walk. It's not on them, it's on me as the leader.

Our practices hadn't been that bad, they just weren't as sharp or intense as we wanted them. And they weren't up to the standard I was constantly talking about. I had to take responsibility for that. There was no way our guys knew the level we needed to practice at, and I had to demand it out of them. I wasn't doing it. As I was making them run, making them toe the line, and making them tuck in their shirts and look me in the eye, I wanted to let them know it was my fault, not theirs. They weren't being punished for their mistakes. They were being trained to be champions. We had to change our approach to get there.

Safety

By taking ownership and admitting my mistakes, I showed the players some vulnerability. Being vulnerable was an aspect I hadn't really thought about, and I since learned it was very important. By admitting my own faults and showing them some vulnerability, I created a safe place in our program, where it was okay to make mistakes. I told my team all the time "No one is going to make more mistakes than I am," but I was going to make sure I owned up to them and I corrected them. I expected them to do the same. This created an environment where our team was not afraid to make mistakes. A safe environment where they could compete without fear.

Competing at a high level isn't naturally a safe thing to do in any organization. Think about it. If you give everything you have and it isn't enough, you have no safety net. You have to admit you weren't good enough. By showing some vulnerability and creating a safe environment, you put your team in a place where they are comfortable letting their guard down. They are willing to give you everything they have, because it's okay to fail. We'll deal with it as a team. To get your team to compete at a high level, safety is very important. You can create safety by showing vulnerability as a leader. That level of safety helped develop the competitive edge that would come to define us.

The Mental Side

That first year as a head coach turned out to be incredibly important to me. I've always felt that starting at a division III school without a lot of money was great for me as a first time head coach. It's a place where you can make mistakes without facing a lot of negative feedback, and one where you learn to do whatever it takes. You sweep the gym floor, you wash the laundry, you go to the bank to cash the meal money check, and your order the pizza after the game. You learn very clearly that you are entitled to nothing.

As we changed the tone of our practices after that trip to West Conn, I learned more about the importance of the mental side of the game. It is so often overlooked and under coached. When you prepare to be a head coach you think about style of play and X's and O's. As I said, I realized when I became a head coach that about 75% of my message to the team was about mentality, preparation, and approach. It wasn't about set plays or spacing. And I'm talking about all of the time—in practices, in games, in huddles, on the court and off. With four minutes to play, in a tight game, most of the conversation was about being mentally tough, staying focused, understanding the situation, and trusting our preparation. It was about the mental game.

Your charge as a leader is to get the most out of the people around you. Of course, you have to know your business very well and show competence to your team. But the environment you create and the relationships you develop are essential to team success. You can know your business cold, but if you don't know your people you won't be leading them for long. Prepare yourself as a leader to understand and coach the mental side. It is the best way to get the most out of the many different personalities you will lead, and very often it is overlooked. As a leader, I spend more time on the mental aspect than I ever expected.

Progress

From the day of our "get the message" practice forward, everything changed. I stayed the course with the new approach and the guys responded. Practices were significantly better, and that was really important to me. I was more demanding, and our compete level was better. Was my team a little bit afraid of me? I'm sure they were, but that wasn't the worst thing in the world. They knew things had to change, and they were willing to invest in something different, something a little uncommon.

And wouldn't you know it, the results started to change. We took out Keene State and UMass-Dartmouth at home. We went on the road and beat Plymouth State and Eastern Connecticut. We hammered Western Connecticut in the rematch at our place by 30. Our guys embraced the new approach and started to see the results. What would have happened if we didn't start to get better results? That's hard to say. I'd like to think we would have continued with the new approach, but I don't know for sure. Success certainly made it easier to stay the course.

It's one of the toughest challenges you'll face as a leader, to demand a high level of accountability when you aren't getting positive results. It's a land mine for effective leadership. One hundred percent belief and commitment in what you are doing is essential, and you have to be mentally prepared for the bumps in the road. If the results aren't there, expect pushback. It's only natural. But it's vital that you stay with it. An inconsistent approach in search of results is a death blow to your culture. Luckily for me, when we made significant changes, we started seeing results.

We won eight of our last nine games after that trip to West Conn to finish up league play. It wasn't like we became a dominant team; we were just more consistent and got a lot more carryover from practice to games. And our confidence started to grow. It wasn't like we thought we were the best team in the league all of the sudden, but it felt right. I got a jolt of confidence for the first time as a head coach. The kids were responding to what we were doing, and I could feel it. It gave me the confidence to keep driving my team the same way.

We finished the regular season 16-8 and 9-5 in the league. We tied for second place and ended up as the three seed in the conference tournament due to the tiebreaker. We were as confident as any team in the league heading into the post-season and our quarterfinal opponent was the six seed—Western Connecticut. We had beaten them easily in our home matchup, and we were able to take them out again in our LEC Tournament game. We had now won nine out of ten and headed to Keene State (the top seed) to take on number two UMass-Boston.

Change the Flow

We had all of the confidence in the world heading up to Keene to play in the semi-finals. We had split with UMass-Boston during the regular season, but the way we were playing we felt like we were good enough to win the tournament. RIC had never before even played in the league championship game.

The semi-final against UMass-Boston was another leadership lesson I learned in the heat of a game. Remember the Wheaton game on opening weekend when I benched Kamari Williams late in the game and we coughed up a lead? The memory of that game probably led to my second big coaching mistake in the semi-finals.

There are certain losses as a head coach you can't shake, and that one will always be one of them for me. I can handle losing, but the games we should win where I feel like I made a mistake to cost us, those I have a hard time with. And this UMass-Boston game was one of those. We went on to play in eight straight NCAA Tournaments after my first year at RIC, and I honestly believe that number should have been nine.

We came out and played very well to start the game. UMass-Boston was very talented, but I thought we were better, and we came into the game playing great. Given the game was at Keene, there was no real home court advantage. Our late-season confidence carried over, and we outplayed them from the jump. We had a double digit lead well into the second half.

With about six minutes to go, we had an 11-point lead and were playing great. UMass-Boston, who had been playing man-to-man the entire game, switched to a 3-2 zone. They hadn't really played zone all year, but they were desperate, and they just tried something different. All they wanted to do was mix it up. They went to a defense they hadn't played all year to see if they could disrupt our flow, and it worked.

It's a good lesson to keep in mind as a leader—to be flexible. Sometimes you just have to try and change things up when they aren't going well to give your opponent a different look. You also give your own team a different feel. The flexibility and confidence to do something different can be a powerful change agent in critical situations.

We didn't handle their zone well, and they started to get stops and chip away at our lead. In a couple of minutes, they had cut it to five, but I still felt confident. We were clearly the better team all night. I had no doubt that we were going to win the game. But we started to get tight when we struggled to score, and Boston gained a lot of confidence in themselves.

Tirrell Hill, our very talented freshman guard who would go on to score 1,000 points in four years, was playing the best game of his young career. He was scoring, setting his teammates up, and playing great defensively. He always played with an edge and a high level of toughness, and he was playing great that night. He was one of our best players.

For the last five minutes, as things got a little tighter, I went with my veteran players. I took Tirrell out and made sure I had Kamari Williams on the floor. There is no doubt I was thinking about that Wheaton game, and how our guys were uncomfortable without Kamari out there. Even though it was clear Tirrell had been our best player and was clearly playing better than Kamari. I let a mistake I made in November impact a decision I made in February.

The Safe Route

Deciding who to count on is a challenge for any coach or leader. Do you go with the veteran performer who has consistently produced over time even when he's not at his best? Or do you go with the young upstart who is starting to produce and has something to prove? While your organization may not have "starters" and "backups," the parallel is still there. How do you effectively use your personnel to get the most for your organization?

One of my toughest challenges as a head coach is when a backup is outplaying one of my starters in a close game. Who do you finish the game with? Most head coaches go with the safe play—and the safe play is to finish the game with your starter. No one is going to question you when you finish the game with your starters. If you lose, it's because they didn't play well. But if you leave your bench guys out there and you lose, you get questioned for your decisions. It's not an easy call in close games. The safe play isn't always the right one, and too often as leaders we default to what is safe.

I went with the safe play that night, and it was the wrong one. I didn't look at who was playing better and who gave us a better chance to win. I thought back to another mistake I had made late in a game, and I tried to correct it. We crumbled down the stretch and lost a game we clearly should have won. When the game ended, Tirrell Hill had only played 12 minutes and scored 16 points. Kamari Williams played 31 minutes and was 3-11. But I finished the game with Kamari on the floor and 'Rell on the bench. It was a huge mistake, and it clearly cost us.

Losing that game was a complete shock. We had failed to handle the defensive change UMass-Boston made late and we got tight. I made a bad personnel decision that really hurt us. There was no doubt in my mind we were headed to play Keene in the championship game for the first time in program history. And we let it slip away.

UMass-Boston went on to beat Keene State in the finals the next day and go to the NCAA Tournament. Keene head coach Rob Colbert was a friend, and he had confided in me that his team was physically exhausted after their semi-final game, and he didn't think they had much left for the final. And he was right. UMass-Boston won easily.

We went on to win two games in the ECAC tournament after that loss, including winning by 40 at Keene State in the semi-finals. We ended up losing to Wheaton (just couldn't shake them) in the finals.

We finished the year 19-10. I didn't realize it then, but everything we had gone through that year had set the foundation for a championship culture. The struggles, the losing, the discovery I made in January and the willingness of our players to embrace change. We had established an approach that would bring us unprecedented success. We didn't make it to the Little East Championship game in 2006. But we would play in the next eight of them – winning six – on our way to eight straight NCAA Tournaments.

Leaders Are Always Learning

Taking over any organization for the first time is a great learning experience, and it's important to see it that way. We all want to have success right away, and we all feel the pressure that comes along with leadership. I was no different. But as I look back on my first year as a head coach, I see the leadership lessons much more clearly. You may not see it that way as it's happening, but the mistakes you make will shape your approach and help you grow.

I learned a great deal that year as a head coach. I honestly think I was the missing piece to what should have been a championship team. I was glad to have my first opportunity at a division III school where no one was really paying too much attention. I could make my mistakes in relative peace, only having to answer to my players. I walked out of the Murray Center many nights after practice thinking, "Well, that didn't work." It was a great benefit to be in that situation in my first year. A chance to learn and grow without intense pressure, other than what I placed on myself. I made a lot of mistakes, but we used them to get better in the long run. I was able to see it as a learning experience, a luxury many leaders do not get.

I had cost our team by not setting the right tone in practice from day one; by not recognizing that things had to be different, simply because I was a new head coach, and embracing that change. I wasn't strong enough with regards to our culture and how we were going to operate day to day. When I finally figured it out, we had already cost ourselves a bunch of games. At 17-9 after the conference tournament we weren't in the mix for an NCAA bid. But at 20-6, we probably had a chance. Had I set the tone properly from day one, could we have won three more games? I think so. We certainly were talented enough.

I'm convinced, knowing what I know now, that we were the best team in the league my first year, and we finished tied for second. But I'm also not sure we would have set the foundation for our long-term culture without the difficulties we had in our first 15 games. I was trying to figure things out as a head coach and find the true strength of my voice. I'm not sure I would have done that had we not lost a bunch of those early games. I went into that off-season confident in what was necessary for us to be successful.

Talent Matters

I also learned a simple truth that is often overlooked when we talk about leadership: talent matters. There isn't a specific leadership formula that works to make bad organizations better, or good organizations great. I know how much we like to stress hard work, discipline and effort and those things certainly are important. But when I'm asked what I look for first in a recruit, my answer is always natural talent. You can culture the heck out of your opponent day after day, but without the necessary talent any leadership approach will struggle to find results.

There is just a certain level of ability necessary to achieve high performance in any field, especially athletics where physical ability is a big factor. Talented players can process things quicker on the move, play at a faster pace comfortably, and utilize their skills under pressure. They allow you to build your culture and refine your approach more easily. They just get it quicker, and the game comes more naturally to them. I'm confident this is the same in most arenas. Talent is a difference maker for great lawyers, great doctors, or great teachers. We love to tell kids at summer camp that if they are fully committed and willing to put in the hard work necessary, they can be anything they want to be. Well, I just don't think that is true. I could have taken ground balls all day, every day but I still don't think I was good enough to be the Yankees short stop. In a lot of ways, I think we glorify hard work (it is obviously a very valuable approach) and therefore downplay the importance of talent. I benefitted a great deal in my first year being surrounded by great talent as I tried to find my leadership voice.

Talent makes it easier to achieve buy-in. While I was trying to find my way as a leader, we were still talented enough to win some games. The players saw some reward for the effort we were putting in. And what I was asking of them was just easier for them to accomplish because they were good enough. Had we been 5-10 in our first 15 games, it would have been a lot tougher to get the buy-in necessary to turn things around. It's simply easier to get buy-in when you are experiencing success.

I learned this for certain when I left RIC in 2014 and became the head coach at the University of Maine. While I took over the best team in the league at RIC, I took over the worst team in the league at Maine—and it wasn't even close. It is great to emphasize and value things like work ethic, commitment, and toughness when building your organization because those are attributes that can be cultivated and developed. But it is much harder to do that when your guys really struggle with what you are asking of them. That's not to say you can't do it and accomplish great things. I'll always be very proud of the culture we developed at Maine despite a lack of wins. But it took us a full four years at Maine to get the culture right. It was simply much tougher with less talent.

Finding the best natural talent that is capable of handling what you need them to do is an important key to success, and one that surprisingly gets overlooked. Life isn't a leadership book. The ability of your people makes a difference.

FIVE

BUILDING ON SUCCESS

APRIL 2006 (THE OFF-SEASON)

One significant difference between an athletic team and many organizations is the off-season. We have a clearly defined season, where we are trying to win games, and off-season, where we are focused on getting better. I recognize that's not the same for every organization, where the ability to improve and accomplish have to coexist all year long.

NCAA rules don't allow for division III coaches to work with their players outside of the season. There are no individual workouts, no conditioning, and generally no summer school. You really can't do anything. The only time you are allowed in the gym with your players is during the season, from the day practice starts (October 15th) until the day your season ends. After that, the players work out on their own.

I'm sure it's quite different in many organizations. We have rules keeping us from working with our players in the off-season. Imagine if at your law firm or your wealth management company that you could only work with your team for half of the year. That's essentially what it's like as a division III basketball coach. I had my team for five months, and they were on their own for seven. As a division I coach I was used to having individual development time in the off-season. It was a challenging adjustment for me especially as we tried to establish our culture.

The Value of Separation

That first off-season wasn't very comfortable for me because I naturally wanted to be in the gym. But I learned an important lesson about building an elite culture: The value of separation.

I couldn't do anything about it, so I decided to embrace it. I wasn't going to be the coach who was peeking into the gym to see who was playing or had a sign-up sheet on his office door for kids who came over to get shots up. We didn't have an off-season workout plan or a summer calendar that the team had to follow. I didn't think it would be effective, and we couldn't require them to do anything per NCAA rules. I decided to put it on them. Another chance to create ownership.

First of all, I didn't call a post-season meeting. I never did. We all needed some time off, and I wanted the players to come back to me when they were ready. After a long, intense season, the last thing our guys needed was me telling them what to do. Usually our season ended somewhere around or on spring break, so our guys got some natural time off. I'd wait for them to come back and get in the gym, which they usually did right away. They'd pop into the office and ask me when they were going to start playing again, when they were going to lift—and I'd ask them the same thing. I asked them what they thought was important in the post-season and I challenged them to handle it. They had to get together with their teammates and figure out what was going to work. The off-season was theirs, not mine.

As our culture really started to take hold, I came to appreciate how important the separation in the offseason was for our success. There is a big difference between a team (or a player) that gets into the gym because they want to do it and one that gets into the gym because they are being told to do it. It's similar to an employee who really believes in the company mission, versus one just following orders. I wanted them to feel the responsibility of getting better, both individually and as a team, and for that to happen I had to give them space.

I believe this wholeheartedly—so much of the championship culture that we established at Rhode Island College developed in the off-season, in the seven months of the year when we didn't have practice. It developed in the recreation center, the weight room, and on the track, when I was nowhere to be found. Our players established how we were going to act, with the guidance of the way we practiced during the season as their compass. They had my voice in the back of their heads, for sure, but their ownership is what really drove our culture.

Meritocracy

That first off-season, as I got them talking about what was important, I made sure to reinforce our standards. If they were going to be on their own for seven months, they had to carry our culture forward.

I made it very clear that our program was a meritocracy. All high achieving organizations are based on merit. Everything was earned and that would never change. What mattered most always was what you had done for us that day. It didn't make a difference if you were a starter last year or an all-league player. The number of minutes you played were unimportant. If you didn't get better and stay in great shape in the off-season, that was on you. Merit was our daily currency.

I emphasized there would always be a lot of talent in our program, and we were going to continue to upgrade that talent. I reminded them I was recruiting over them. I made no bones about it. My job was always to find better players for the program. Their job was to get better.

Define merit for your organization and make sure you adhere to those standards. For us it meant three things— compete, produce,

61

and be a great teammate. Those were the standards that earned merit in our program and we defined them that offseason. Give a great effort every day, make that effort productive for our team, and put the team and your teammates first. If you did those three things, you'd earn your way as a player. As always, we defined behaviors that represented those standards. The only difference in the off-season was they'd be on their own, without coaching supervision. They had to hold one another accountable.

Merit is the currency exchanged within high performing teams. Determine what merit means for yourself first, before applying it to your organization. What are the simple standards you want your people to be accountable to every day? Make sure they are important to you, and that you personally can live up to them. Then define merit for your team and hold them accountable as well. Everything is earned. You'll create the right mentality throughout your team.

The Mission

While I was happy with the progress made in year one and I knew we had a good team coming back, I still thought we lacked a real championship mentality. While we believed in each other and the culture we were developing, I'm not sure we really knew what it took to be great. Remember, RIC was the program that had some talent but always found a way to lose in the big spots. And I was sure that mentality was still ingrained in our program in some ways, because we once again lost in big spots—in the semi-final game up vs. UMass-Boston, and in the post-season ECAC final at home against Wheaton. My goal that off-season was to change the way we thought —and start to develop a championship mentality.

I don't think you change the mentality with one seismic event. I think it starts with language, with conversations, and with daily affirmations of little things. It's simply about establishing the right way to do things, on and off the court. Granted, a big moment can certainly make an impact, but you have to instill belief day to day before you get to that moment. Establishing a mentality is like water flowing over a rock. With continued persistence, the rock eventually starts to smooth out. Working on our mentality was my main focus of the off-season.

I felt we needed a clearly defined mission to get everyone on board. There is a famous story about President Kennedy visiting NASA after he charged them with putting a man on the moon in the 1960s. The President introduced himself to a janitor in the hallway and asked him what he did at NASA. His response was "I'm here to put a man on the moon, Mr. President." Everyone in the building, from the janitors to the engineers, was on the same mission.

I wanted our guys to have the same mindset, so I asked them what their mission was. Most of them talked about winning championships. Championships are great, but they are really a goal, not necessarily a mission. I asked them if that was enough, if it was just about winning for them. If that were the case, did we not accomplish anything that year because we fell short of a championship? They started to talk about doing things every day at a championship level. It went beyond winning championships, to carrying ourselves at a championship level all the time.

"Championship level, everything we do."

That's the mission we came up with. Five words that would define our approach every day. We would talk constantly about what a championship level looked like and we defined the behaviors—both on the court and off—that lived up to that standard. It was as simple as asking "Is that a championship level?" to remind everyone what was expected. "Championship level, everything we do" became our unified mission and helped solidify our mentality.

Defining a mission gives your organization a simple way to define your approach. It's something your team can discuss, embrace and fight for when necessary. It shouldn't be complicated, but it's more than just "that's not how we do things." It should be something they think about when no one is watching, when they are being counted on by their teammates to get the job done. A defined mission can be very powerful for your leadership approach.

Listen to Your Team

Without being in the gym in the off-season, I had to be intentional about affecting our mentality. As I mentioned, I always learned the most about my team when I listened to them. And if I wanted our mentality to change, I had to communicate with them constantly. I made sure to get feedback from them just about every day.

This started with casual conversation, when really that was the only contact I could have with my players. They would fill me in on what was going on with the team, who was doing well and who was struggling, and what we could do better. All I had to do was ask. I can't stress enough the importance of these conversations with your team. Not only are you developing relationships that cement the level of trust, much of your mentality is created organically, through conversation. The more you listen, the more you succeed.

Listening is the most underdeveloped leadership skill. A leadership mistake I see a lot is thinking we have to be the one telling others what to do. If you listen to your team you'll learn so much about them, and the insight will make you a better leader. Ask questions and give them the safety to speak honestly. Mentality can be created through listening if you have the self-discipline to do it.

Changing a Losing Mentality

One thing that gnawed at me that first season was the way we played on the road. We looked like a different team in someone else's gym, and I attributed it to our mentality. It was a glaring example of the need for improvement in our mental approach.

When we went up to Keene State to play our first league game that year, they really impressed me. We were down by one point at halftime, 49-48, and we had played really well. We couldn't sustain it in the second half, and we lost the game by 15. They were one of the best teams in the league and they'd end up winning it. We had given them our best shot, and they handled us pretty well.

Fast forward six weeks when Keene came to RIC for the rematch. I was worried about the game, even though we were playing well at the time. I thought Keene was better than us. But the ball went up and we handled them pretty easily, controlling the game from start to finish. We played well, but the game didn't have near the same level of intensity as our first meeting up at Keene. They were a different team on the road than they were at home.

I realized after that game our team was very similar. We were a different team on the road. We just didn't have the same edge. We traveled the day of the game, and for league games we rode with the women's team. That meant leaving in the morning on a Saturday, spending somewhere between 1-3 hours on a bus, and arriving around 11:30 (the women would play at 1:00) for a game that didn't start until 3:00. It could be a long day, especially for the longer trips in the league (although trust me I'm not complaining—try the bus trips at the University of Maine on for size).

What I realized was that most teams—the Anchormen included— were different on the road. And I didn't think the bus rides had much to do with it. It was a mentality. It felt like we were supposed to lose on the road, because we thought it was really hard. Losing on the road felt acceptable in our league, and in our program. I hated that mentality. It was a concrete example of the mentality change I wanted to see in that first off-season.

Luckily, I had the perfect scenario to use to try and change it. That spring I had talked to a good friend, Jeff Ruland, who was the head coach at Iona College in New York, about playing them in an exhibition game. I thought it would be a great opportunity for our program to play a division I team, and it would force us to prepare at a high level. It was also a road game to start our season, one that I could use to help change our mentality.

After we signed to play the game, I talked to our team about opening with an exhibition game at Iona the next year. They were naturally excited to play a division I team. But I made sure to tell them very clearly something they would hear in some version quite often that spring. We weren't going down there to play an exhibition. We were going down there to win the game.

My basic message that day was this: I would not have scheduled the game if I didn't think we were good enough to win it. But our mentality when we get on the bus has to change. We aren't going down there to give them a good fight or help them get a workout in before their season starts. We are going down there to win the game. We have to establish a new mentality in this program. When we get on the bus, no matter where we go, we get on the bus expecting to win the game. Everything we do in practice every day prepares us to win tough games against good teams on the road. We are going to prepare that way, and when we get on the bus we expect to win. No other mentality is acceptable.

From that moment on, I never used the term "on the road" with my team again. We often made too big of a deal out of playing on the road, to the point where it became self-fulfilling. We talked a lot about how hard it was to win on the road, and we started to believe it. I never used phrases like "especially on the road" in a scouting report. If we are doing our job as a program, the way we practice every day is preparing us to handle tough crowds, great teams and bad breaks from the officials. We are preparing to win on the road. We didn't need to talk about it. It's not like when we played at home, I showed up feeling like the game would be easy. Winning is hard anywhere. Convincing your guys that winning on the road is harder just gives them a subconscious excuse to use as a crutch. I wanted to eliminate that in our mentality.

As a leader I wanted to be honest, but I also had to be careful about giving my team a convenient excuse. The more you talk about how hard something is going to be, the more they come to believe it. We are all preparing for the difficult challenges we will face as a team every day. Your team needs to hear how prepared they are, not how difficult things will be. Avoid planting the seeds of defeatist mentality. It can be very subtle, but also very powerful.

All spring we talked about going to Iona and winning. The way we prepared would create a mentality that when we got on the bus, we expected to win. That was going to be the new standard in our program.

In my nine years at RIC we were 84-38 on the road. My first year we were 6-8. After that first off-season, and our intentional change in mentality, we were 78-30.

Accountability Everywhere

That off-season gave me a lot of time to reflect, and I learned another important leadership lesson. Unfortunately, it came out of a difficult situation.

When I left the Big East to take the RIC job, different people told me how challenging roster management was at the D3 level. There really wasn't much you could do about it, they said, because the kids aren't on scholarship. Kids are going to come and go a lot, and you can't really hold them accountable. Especially when it came to academics. Kids were going to fail off and your roster was going to be different after Christmas every year – that's just the way it worked.

I didn't want to accept that. When I took over, I made sure our guys knew we were going to go to class. That is where the accountability in our program started, with your 8 AM class on Monday morning. I would be out there a couple of times each week in the morning to make sure they were on time for class. That was the deal.

I was going to hold them accountable academically simply because it was the right thing to do. I wanted them to be successful in the classroom and to get a degree, and I also wanted our roster to remain stable. What I didn't realize was how much the academic accountability would make me a much better coach. By delivering that message early and following through on it, the guys knew I was sincere. I meant what I said. It helped establish (eventually) that the message was not negotiable.

As we got further along into the season, and certainly year after year, I could actually see the impact on the court. By January and February our guys realized that when I delivered a message, I was going to follow through on it. There was no indecision. When we talked about basketball decisions, how we were going to practice, or game plans, there were no questions in their mind. If this is how we said we were going to play a ball screen, there was no indecision. I could literally see and feel the trust our guys had on the court. It all started with the accountability that came with the academics in the fall. Our trust as a team started off the court.

Accountability was a big part of our championship culture, and a big part of any long term, sustained success. Again, for us it was about a responsibility to the behaviors that upheld our core values. But it's so much more than the decisions you make in games or in practice. It's something your team needs to see everywhere. In fact, it's probably more impactful when it's away from the gym. Getting to class, getting your work in, study hall, just simply being on time — accountability is everywhere. Your team needs to see that is how you live your life—and when they do, they'll start to believe in your decisions.

Accountability should be present everywhere in your organization. It's not just a discipline you find when things get *really* important. Don't ever take short cuts with accountability. If you do, the foundation of your program will never be strong enough.

Culture Over Talent

For many the word culture represents a shared set of beliefs. But for us, culture was the behavior that represented those beliefs. Again, it was about actions, not words.

From the start of our first year we had a standard for going to class – "Every class, on time, up front, phones off." It was that simple. We were going to every class, we would be on time, we were sitting up front and our phones were off. The expected behavior was very clear, and there was no gray area. To be honest, I was probably a little bit maniacal about it when we first started. But I was trying to establish a way of doing things. If you didn't go to class, we were having a team meeting at 7 AM the following day. After we reinforced the message first thing in the morning, the guys would finish the meeting on the court with some conditioning. They would come to learn it wasn't worth the risk to miss class. They would start to hold each other accountable for it—another great sign of ownership.

We also had a very strict study hall policy at RIC, one that really scared me at first. Study hall was run by the athletic director and was monitored by athletic department staff. The coaches had nothing to do with it. Every player who was either a first year student or had below a 3.0 GPA had to complete eight hours of study hall by Thursday night at 8 PM, and if you didn't complete your hours you were immediately ineligible. You were done. You could not practice or play for a week, until you were able to make up your hours by the following Thursday.

I originally thought that was way too strict, and I figured we'd lose guys all the time. But the truth is it made us better. Everyone knew there was no wiggle room whatsoever with study hall and you couldn't come to the coaching staff to plead your case. We had no control over it. The guys made sure they didn't screw it up, or they couldn't play for a week. It was another area where strict accountability off the court helped us get better on the court.

At first there were obviously challenges with the new approach. Many of our guys came to me and said no one had ever really cared if they went to class or not in the past. It's not like they adapted to it right away and things went very smoothly. We had our share of 7 AM meetings that first year.

A few weeks into the post-season we had a couple of players miss class, so we called a 7 AM meeting in the recreation center. Guys weren't happy. I'm sure they were upset at me because they thought the season was over and they weren't going to have to deal with this anymore. But they were also upset at their teammates for putting them in that position. Tension was pretty high, as it usually was when you made college kids get up at the crack of dawn for conditioning.

I made the message very clear, that it didn't matter whether or not we were in season. Championship level, everything we do. We were going to go to class. Accountability just isn't something you do some of the time. The guys got on the court and started to run, but it was very clear they were unhappy. They were bitching at each other the entire way. After a couple of minutes, I went back in the gym and pulled the guys together again.

I let them know I really wasn't happy with their response and lit into them pretty good. Now I was upset. I made it clear that this was how our program was going to be run. We were going to go to class, we were going to be held accountable, and that was how we were going to win championships. If any of them didn't like it, they could leave.

And then I heard, "Man, this is some bullshit. I'm out of here."

One of our sophomores on that year's team, Benjy Nichols, spoke up. He was a talented kid who I loved as a player and a teammate. He was smart and tough, not to mention a great athlete and he was a no-nonsense person. He had come off the bench for that year's team but was a valuable player who figured to be a starter and a key contributor before his career was over. He was exactly the kind of player I wanted on my team. And he walked away. He went over to the baseline, grabbed his bag, and walked out of the gym. The rest of the team stood there staring at me.

I can still remember how empty my stomach felt. I was scared. What happens if the rest of the team walks away right now as well? What do I do then? I was worried I might have a coup on my hands. I froze for a second, not exactly sure how this was going to play out.

I'll always remember that day as one of the most important in my career as a young head coach. I had just finished my first year and I had gone all in with our culture on accountability. I had gone after my guys pretty hard that morning to make the point. They were pissed. And now one of our key players, and a respected veteran, was challenging me and walking away. In front of the entire team.

"Anybody else?" I said defiantly as I watched him walk away. But trust me, I was pretty nervous. I was afraid a bunch of guys might leave, but hopefully I didn't show it. I waited for about 10 seconds in silence and the guys just stared at me. My message was clear – you were either in or you were out – and I didn't really care who you were. My stomach was in knots about what might happen next, but with all of the work we had done on accountability and building our culture, I went all in. If you show your team any sign of weakness with regards to your culture, they will pounce on it. I wasn't going to do that.

Luckily for me, no one else moved. I was still nervous, but I felt a little better because no one else had decided to walk away.

"We will go to class, we will be on time, we will sit up front, and we will have our phones off. If you can't do that, you can't be a part of this. We are building something special here. If you don't want to be a part of it, walk away now." With that the meeting was over and the guys went to class.

Benjy Nichols never played another game for me at Rhode Island College, and to be honest that is something I regret. He was a great kid and I loved coaching him. We kept track of him academically and made sure he was still going to class, and he did graduate from Rhode Island College. He's someone I still have great respect for and consider him a part of our program. His high school coach still thanks me for helping him graduate, which I greatly appreciate because after his sophomore year he never played another minute.

I learned a very valuable lesson that day: You have to be willing to sacrifice talent for your culture. We lost a very talented player that day who was a good kid and fit in well. But he challenged me, and in essence our culture, in front of the entire team. You cannot accept that within your organization. If our culture really mattered the way I said it did, we had to let him go. Talent matters, absolutely. But you can replace talent. It's really hard to repair holes in your culture.

I have no doubt that our team's belief in how we went about our business got stronger that day. Our culture was growing, and accountability was part of our core. The message was clear and direct, and it would not be disregarded, whether it was showing up on time the day of the West Conn game or going to class in April. That was a significant day in the formation of our culture and the dynasty we were building.

SIX

THE PRESSURE OF LEADERSHIP

SEPTEMBER 2006 (THE START OF YEAR TWO)

A s we headed into the fall to start our second year, we continued to work on our championship mentality. We would have most of the team coming back (we only lost KP to graduation) and we added a couple of talented newcomers, but the core was still intact. It was time to put it all together, and a lot of pressure came with that.

Values in Behavioral Terms

Our meritocracy was in place. What have you done for the program today? That is what really mattered. Compete, produce and be a great teammate. That was RIC basketball.

Those standards were our core values, and we continued to define them as behavior. Our values needed to be more than talk. I had to make it clear to my team what the actions were that defined our values and show the behaviors we expected. Values are more than signs on the wall or phrases on the back of your shooting shirts. They have to be behaviors that your team can understand and perform.

Competing was the foundation of what we did on and off the court every day. But it had to be more than me yelling at them to compete when I didn't like what was going on—it needed to be connected to action. When someone dove on the floor for a loose ball, we celebrated it. That's competing. When someone sprinted back in transition to get a deflection and stop a fast break, we celebrated it. Competing. When you got up early to get extra study hall hours in because you had a big test that day, that's competing. Your best effort always, without compromise, was competing to us and we made those behaviors clear.

It was important to me to emphasize production as one of our standards, even though you may think it goes without saying. Production matters. If all we talked about was who competed the hardest and did the right thing, we could end up with a really hard-working group that wasn't very good. Effort and commitment are really important, and they are the things we can control. But it's not enough. In any organization, the ability to produce should be celebrated. I'd never say that I'm going to start my five hardest workers, or my five best competitors, because it's just not true. You will coach guys who compete their ass off on every possession but struggle to score or get rebounds. And you'll coach guys who play smooth and casual but can get you 15 points. Believe it or not, production is actually something that is often undervalued. We have an idea in our head as a coach what a good player looks like and we get caught up in stuff like length and athleticism that represents potential, yet we often overlook production. Everything you like about your personnel should add up to production for your organization. If it doesn't you probably shouldn't like it so much.

Finally, we wanted great teammates. This value was very general, and that was on purpose. Being a great teammate encapsulates so many different things, on and off the court. If you show up every day and sacrifice your personal goals for the team, that's being a great teammate. It involves being a good player, but also being a good person. It's a broad way of making sure your guys are doing the right thing. But again, you have to define the behaviors for them. Reminding guys to get their study hall hours in. Calling guys to make sure they are awake before an early morning practice. Walking guys away from a party if a fight is about to go down. There are a lot of ways to define for your team what it means to be a great teammate.

Compete, produce, and be a great teammate. That was how you earned merit in our program.

Defining values as behaviors is an effective way to turn talk into action. Make sure everyone in your organization knows not only what your core values are, but what they look like as behavior. Terms like work ethic, commitment, and loyalty are pretty hollow if they aren't attached to something real. Define and celebrate the behaviors connected to your core values and they become essential elements of your culture.

Ready to Adapt

When we first got together as a team in September of 2006, we had a lot of talent and experience. This was my first recruiting class as a head coach—I got the job in September of 2005—so it was the first time I had to bring together newcomers with returning players. We had a newcomer that year—Bobby Bailey, who would go on to be the Little East Player of the Year in 2009—who I knew was going to be very good. But we also had most of our production back from the year before. My challenge that year was building a cohesive team with new talent that was going to push our veteran players.

I learned starting with that meeting that I was really building a new team. Every year is different. Sure, some years are easier than others when you have a lot of returning players, but the dynamics are new, even if you have most of your key people back. We had experienced some success as a group, but we fell short of our championship goal. Four of our key players were now sophomores, having contributed while figuring out life as freshmen in college. Six of our veteran players were now seniors, facing their last year. They had all experienced different levels of individual success—from playing time to awards, starting games to coming off the bench. Coming back in

2006, things were different for all of them. They had new expectations for themselves with the experience of that year under their belt. We also had a very talented newcomer who figured to play a lot. And things were different for me as well. I was no longer a rookie head coach, trying to figure out what might work and what wouldn't. I was confident in my approach with a better understanding of how my team would respond to my leadership.

This is true for every organization, and something that is easy to overlook. Everyone gets older, everyone experiences different levels of success, and everyone sets different goals. The organization evolves as well, adding new pieces and processes, and along with that come different expectations. A new year brings with it a new team, even if it's the same faces. No matter how much success you are having the beginning of every year is a fresh challenge. If you aren't ready to adapt, you will fall behind the curve. Your personnel will grow every year, as will you. Maintaining the status quo is not a path to consistent, elite achievement. Expect things to be different and embrace the changes you need to make, even if you are experiencing success. You will never lead the same team twice.

Transparency

As always, in our first team meeting of the new year, I was straight up with our guys. I told them that nothing we had done the year before mattered. What was relevant was what we did today. We had no returning starters, no senior leaders, no leading scorers. This team hadn't played a game yet. To think we were all going to step back into the same roles was unrealistic. We were going to see who got better and who was in great shape. It was day one, time to earn your way. This was a meritocracy.

It was kind of raw and direct, but it was the truth. And it was in line with our core values. Trust is essential on great teams, and you can't develop it without being completely transparent. You are not fooling your team. To get the most out of them, be relentlessly transparent. They will believe in you a lot more if you tell them the truth—even if it's not the news they want to hear—than if you dance around it. And people who believe in you will give you everything they have. Find a comfort level with being transparent and your team will respond positively.

Our program was about high level talent competing at a championship level. I was fortunate to inherit the talent. Our guys appreciated the direct nature of our approach, and they loved the competitive edge it represented. It was a true meritocracy, and a siren call to raise your game. If you were afraid to compete, you were in the wrong room.

High Expectations

The exhibition game at Iona was still on our mind when we began in the fall. As we talked about winning the game, I came to understand the importance of the high expectations the game represented. It established an elite compete level in the pre-season and a mentality where we would not back down to anyone. We knew what we were up against, and as we openly talked about getting on the bus to go win the game, our preparation and focus became more acute.

I love when expectations are high. I am not comfortable in a low expectations environment. As I said, I rarely, if ever, talked about winning with my team but our approach to that Iona game was different. Based on what I had learned our first year about our approach when going on the road, I knew we needed to be mentally tougher. So, that fall we kept reinforcing the same message—we are going to Iona to win the game. We needed to understand what winning looked like on a day to day basis before the games started to dominate our mindset. It's one of the rare times where we actually talked about winning as a group, and it isn't lost on me that it was a key moment in building a culture that would rarely if ever talk about winning again.

That Iona game helped set high expectations for our program and made me a big believer in doing so. I want to embrace high expectations. I want everyone around our program to expect us to be champions, especially my players. Dealing with that environment is a challenge for sure, but handling your surroundings is part of being great. I firmly believe that environment brings out the best in most of us, and it eliminates those who can't handle it. You learn faster who you can win with. Give me high expectations all day long. I'd much rather deal with them and plan for success.

Adversity

That pre-season went well. We had a mature group that understood we had a chance to do something special, and a clear attainable goal in winning our league for the first time in school history. We were deep and for the most part healthy. We had one significant injury, to Kamari Williams who had a back problem and wasn't ready to go to start the season. He would not play at Iona. But it solved the dilemma for me that I had screwed up at the end of last season in the Little East Tournament. There was no decision to be made. Tirrell Hill had to play.

My approach to injuries is admittedly pretty cold. I just don't ever want our players to use injuries as an excuse, so I make sure I don't make a big deal out of them. If we are doing our job, we've got a lot of guys prepared to play. It's a big part of our "Win Anyway" approach. When somebody goes down in practice, I don't make a big deal out of it. In fact, I hardly acknowledge it. I don't want practice to stop and have everyone spend two minutes feeling sorry for their teammate. We get the trainer out there, make sure he's okay, and we move on. I don't want my guys thinking that an injury might have a significant impact on the way we operate.

At the end of practice, if we are down some guys to injury, we run an extra sprint for each guy that is out. It doesn't have to be long or challenging. The mentality is we all have to be a little better if we are shorthanded, but we are still going to get the job done. It also keeps guys from sitting out late in practice with a minor injury because they don't want to run. If you can't run, we are going to run for you. It will get guys up on the line for their teammates quickly.

Of course, I make sure that the injured player knows we are going to take care of him. It's not like I freeze out injured players and don't talk to them. Injuries happen and I don't blame them on the players. But I don't want our team to react to them. I don't want it to affect the rest of practice or our next game. They happen, we put someone else in, and we move on.

Handling adversity the right way is situational. I'm not sure there's a blueprint for it. But one thing I don't want to do is make too big of a deal out of the situation. As the leader it's my job to prepare the team for adversity – we know it is coming. It can't be something you just react to when it happens. Whether it's temporary or long term, adversity can have a huge mental impact on your team. And they are going to follow your lead. It's inevitable and if you don't have a plan it can have a big impact on your team.

Later in my career at RIC, this mentality helped us get to the Sweet 16. It was my sixth year and we were playing in the NCAA Tournament in Oswego, NY. We won our first game on Friday night pretty easily, and we got up for breakfast the next morning ready to play the host, SUNY-Oswego, to get to the Sweet 16. As we sat down for breakfast, Mike Akinrola, our first team All-League center, came limping into the breakfast room holding one of his sneakers. He said he could barely walk, and he didn't know what happened to his foot. But he couldn't put any pressure on it. My stomach dropped. Everyone looked up from their breakfast and stared at Big Mike, looking like their dog had just died. There was no air in the room.

We had no idea what happened to Mike, and we got the trainer on it, but he couldn't put his shoe on. He clearly wasn't going to play. We took the bus over to the gym for our morning gameday practice, and everybody was dead silent. There was no excitement or energy about the game we were going to play. I knew I had to wake our team up. There was no way we were going to win that night with everyone feeling sorry for themselves. It was everything I didn't want when an injury happened – the entire team staring at it, wondering what was wrong, feeling like we had no chance to win.

When we got together in our huddle before practice, I was very direct.

"Do you guys know what next Friday is? The Sweet 16. We are playing tonight with a chance to go to the Sweet 16. And they are holding it next Friday, whether we are there or not, so we have to make a decision. Are we going to be there, or not? That's on us. Mike's not going to play tonight. Carl will start alongside Darius up front, and we may have to play smaller at times, so some of the guards are going to have to guard up. But the Sweet 16 is being played next weekend whether Mike plays or not. No one is going to care who was hurt and who wasn't a week ago. We will either be there, or we won't."

I needed to snap our guys out of it, and it worked. We forgot about Mike and we got on with it. Darius Debnam, our starting four-man, moved over to play center and had a career night with 16 points. Carl Lee who was a talented swing forward off the bench, started at the four. We played very well that night, beat Oswego and moved on to the Sweet 16. It was one of our better team wins in my nine years at RIC.

I knew we were still good enough to win, although losing Mike was a huge blow. But the biggest issue was our mindset, and that's what I wanted to address. We weren't going to talk about Mike's injury or spend a minute feeling sorry for ourselves. We were one game away from the Sweet 16, and I wanted to get our mind right. There are no accommodations made on the bottom line for misfortune.

Adversity hits every organization, and you must prepare for it. Your mentality towards the small things that happen day to day makes a big difference. If you make a big deal out of the bad breaks, your team will follow your approach. How your team handles adversity says a lot about the culture of your organization.

Prepare to Win
November 3rd, 2006

Playing Iona in an exhibition game meant a lot to our program, but it also had significant personal meaning for me. Iona was where I grew up. Both of my parents were graduates, and it's where I got my master's degree when I was a graduate assistant after I first got out of school. I went to Jim Valvano's and Pat Kennedy's basketball camps there as a kid. The Gaels were the first college basketball team I ever rooted for. It was home.

The long term mentality shift—"we are getting on the bus to win the game"—seemed like it was starting to take hold, but there was really no way to tell. We had repeated it so much, and I have no doubt it affected our practice habits. Part of playing a division I team in an exhibition game is that your guys really want to win, but part of it no doubt is that they don't want to get embarrassed. Our standards that pre-season had been—everything we did had to be good enough to beat a division I team, one that was coming off a championship season and an NCAA Tournament appearance.

Our mentality heading down to New Rochelle was clear and simple —to win the game. I was confident our guys had bought into the approach. But were we actually good enough to win the game? That I couldn't say. I knew we were prepared to win, and I felt good about that.

When we got to Iona, they didn't really seem prepared for us. A student worker brought us into a very small area that they used as their track locker room, and it was full of bags and gear. There was hardly any room. As our guys tried to figure out where to change, a few Iona track athletes came in from the shower, looking to get to their lockers to change. They were surprised to see a basketball team in their space. I knew the AD at Iona at the time, so I went and found him. I asked him if they could find us a different space. We really didn't have enough room. They took us upstairs and let us use the weight room. It was a big space, with no lockers, no seats or benches. Our guys were pretty sure when they hosted division I opponents they didn't have to dress in the weight room. But, Win Anyway. It was perfect. A little extra "they don't respect us" didn't hurt.

As we made our way onto the floor to warmup, I bumped into Vin Parise, an assistant on the Iona staff who I knew. We caught up about a few things casually and he asked me about my team. He said, "you guys had a pretty good year last year, right?" It was pretty clear they hadn't done much preparation. Then he said, "I can already see it, you guys are going to come out playing hard as hell, you'll be up like 5-4 at the first media timeout and my boss is going to be screaming at us like crazy." I just kind of chuckled.

At that point most of the Iona guys were gathering next to us before taking the floor to warmup, and I remember hearing one of their players say to his teammates, "Let's blow these fools out so we don't have to run at all tomorrow." They didn't seem to have any sense that we might actually be able to play with them.

I looked at my friend Vin and said, "Just so you know, we're pretty serious, man. We can play."

Belief

At halftime we were up 46-24. That is not a misprint. We didn't just show Iona we could play, or that we might win, we were smashing them. Our guys played with a ton of confidence, like we expected to win. It was a terrific effort from a mentality standpoint. We executed our offense, and we were together and connected on defense. We struggled turning the ball over with Iona's length and athleticism causing some problems, but we never got frustrated. We moved on to the next play. When we took care of the ball, we got great looks, and we buried them. Iona really couldn't get good shots against us. It was a thumping.

Halftime was amazing, a moment I will never forget. Our kids went up to the weight room and bounced around with a ton of energy and excitement. I didn't really want to say too much, because we were playing great, but I knew I had to reign our guys in a little bit. What do you say when your team is playing lights out and drilling a division I team by 22 points? I wanted to maintain the energy but also bring them back to reality.

I knew Iona would come out and press us and use their quickness and length to cause more turnovers, and we'd have to be ready. But mostly I wanted our guys to stay focused. "We came here to win the game. The most meaningless numbers in your life are the halftime score. No one cares. Go out there ready to attack them. To win the game." I wanted to make sure we stayed aggressive. Twenty minutes was a lot of time and the last thing I wanted to do was try and protect the lead.

Iona came out and got after us like we knew they would, and their pressure bothered us. At one point they cut the lead to three. But we continued to play hard, stay together, and we played to win. We handled their pressure well enough and made winning plays down the stretch.

RIC 77, Iona 71. And it wasn't that close.

We didn't play a perfect game or knock in 15 three-pointers. We didn't do anything statistically outrageous—although we did commit 30 turnovers! But that night we were prepared, composed, and certainly the tougher team. There was no question we deserved to win.

I'll never forget the smile on my Dad's face in the hallway after that game. He was an Iona alum who stayed heavily involved with the school over the years, at one time the President of the Alumni Association and the Athletic Goal Club. He's in their athletic hall of fame. And he'd never been so thrilled to see his alma mater lose. I lost my Dad a few years later to a heart attack, and I have so many great memories of our relationship and time we spent together. The smile on his face after that game is a memory I'll cherish forever.

Challenge Your Team

Winning the Iona game taught me the value of challenging my team. To achieve consistent success, put your team in a position where they know you need their absolute best on a daily basis. Force them to prepare at an elite level. And let them know you believe in them. We did a lot of things right in preparing for that Iona game, but what was most important was the mentality we created. I told them as soon as they knew about the game that I expected to win it. I challenged them at a high level, and they knew I believed in them.

It was also a lesson in "learning how to win" that I referenced earlier. The misconception is that we learned how to win at Iona that night, and that is not the case. We learned how to win every day in that pre-season when we altered our mentality and took a championship approach to preparation. When the lights aren't on, well before the ball goes up – that is when teams learn how to win.

While winning that game was an incredible feeling—and it would help transform our program—challenging our team at that level wasn't really about winning. We did go on to beat Holy Cross the following year (how many D3s have won back to back games against D1 teams?), and we would go on to play the University of Rhode Island and Providence College the following years, without another win. But preparing for games at that level became a part of our DNA and set the tone for our pre-season every year. It was a great way to challenge my team.

There was another funny story from that night at Iona I will never forget. We did our fair share of recruiting in New York, so when we scheduled Iona, my assistants connected with some of our recruits to get them to come watch us play. Matt O'Brien, the first assistant I ever hired, was recruiting a 6-5 kid from a private school in New York City named Jack Robbins. He wanted to be a film major, and on the way down to the game, Matt was talking to him about our fine arts department and how Providence was a great city for the performing arts. He and his Mom were going to come to the game.

After the game, Matt introduced me to Jack and his mother in the hallway, and after about 15 seconds I saw everyone around me smiling wide. And then I realized I was talking to Susan Sarandon, the actress. Her husband was Tim Robbins, and Jack was their son. We had no idea through the beginning of the recruiting process that Jack Robbins was the son of two of the most famous actors of the day. And Matt was trying to sell him on our fine arts program at Rhode Island College. Susan Sarandon could not have been any nicer, and she told me that when the Iona people realized she was there they introduced themselves to her and offered her and Jack some Iona gear. She politely declined, saying, "No thank you, we are actually here to watch Rhode Island College." Go Anchormen.

We didn't land Jack as a recruit to RIC. He must have found some better connections to get into the film business. But it did add a surreal ending to an unbelievable night.

The Power of a Moment

November 3rd, 2006 was not just a special night for all of us at RIC, it might be the most important night in my career as a coach. Remember, I took over a program that supposedly couldn't win a big game. We had started talking about winning that game in April, and everything we focused on for the next six months was about going down there to win. And we did it.

Heading into that season, I felt like we were moving in the right direction, but I wasn't sure how much we really *believed*. Truthfully, there was still some doubt in my own mind. The Iona win gave our team a ton of confidence, but it also established a belief in what we were doing every day—a lot of which was hard and uncommon.

Our practices were intense and tough, and an adjustment for most of our players.

Personally, that night gave me all of the confidence I needed as a coach. It validated everything I believed in, and everything I was trying to establish at RIC. The level we competed at, what we demanded out of our guys, the accountability, the discipline, all of it. That night gave me rock solid credibility with my players and all the confidence I needed as the leader.

I used the word "uncommon" with our players a lot because I knew we were asking a lot of them. We challenged them to compete with intensity all of the time, and there was no let up. It wasn't easy, but elite success is not easy, nor is it convenient. Success doesn't really have options, it has requirements. That fall, our guys understood what the requirements looked like, and they felt what it was like to be rewarded.

At times early in my career, I wondered if it was working, or if what we were doing was too tough. Those doubts are natural. From that night on, whenever I had those doubts, I'd think about that night at Iona. I knew it was worth it, and I knew it worked.

That night had a huge impact on the buy-in to my leadership approach. The problem is those moments are hard to create. It has to happen naturally, through your approach and mentality. That night will always be the night I really started believing in my leadership approach, and more importantly my players did as well. You can "create" those key moments every day with a relentless pursuit of progress.

SEVEN

HANDLING SUCCESS

NOVEMBER 2006

N ow what?

We started out my second year as a head coach with a talented, veteran team and high expectations. We then went on the road and knocked off a division I team. So how do you handle that success when you get back to campus? I'll tell you what, I had no idea. I really didn't.

Obviously, the confidence we took from beating Iona was important to everyone – our players and our coaching staff. But I failed to adequately prepare our team mentally after we won that game. As important as our approach was leading up to that game, I didn't recognize the importance of it after we won. Up to that point, I had never really thought about handling success. You win, things are going well, you just keep it going and everything will be great, right? Well, I learned pretty quickly that doesn't work. My team had great confidence, but after that win everything changed. Our expectations, the way people looked at us, the way we looked at ourselves, it was all different. Handling success is something you have to prepare for intentionally, and it can be harder than handling failure.

The Tension of Expectations

The strongest emotion I felt in our gym after we got back from Iona was tension. We were loose and confident on the outside, sure, and we felt good about ourselves. But things had clearly changed, and our team, including myself, was really tight. Winning that game had raised expectations, and rightfully so. I love high expectations, and I want them around my program all the time. But there can be a lot of tension around teams with high expectations, and I wasn't ready to deal with it.

When we got back from Iona, we expected perfection. It's not like we talked about it – it's just how it felt. Every time someone made the smallest mistake, everyone jumped on him. We weren't allowed to drop a pass, or forget a play, or miss an open teammate. Even when we executed well, it wasn't good enough. It was expected. It was an odd feeling because we expected to feel great. You'd think we'd come back flying, excited, and upbeat, and in some ways we did. There was a lot of energy, and our guys were going hard. But our practices were very tight. You could feel the tension, as if we were never allowed to make a mistake. It was not a good place to be.

After experiencing the success at Iona, I needed to recognize things were going change. There was a strong, confident energy around our team, but expectations were different. I needed to talk to my team about how we felt, and I didn't. We needed a game plan to respond. The most important thing would have been just to recognize that things would be different. As a leader, I learned the hard way that you need to prepare to handle success.

Celebrate

Something else that is important to remember is to celebrate. And I'm not talking about going out after the big moment and having a few drinks. I'm talking about day to day, after you get back to work, to remember to celebrate your daily achievements. As we raised expectations with our win at Iona, I started to take the positives for granted. If we executed really well to score, well, we were supposed to do that. If someone made a great defensive effort, that was just what we did. It was expected, not celebrated. I spent a lot more time focused on the negatives than the positives, and we started to take the positive for granted. Acknowledging and celebrating small, day-to-day success is really important. I overlooked that, because I wasn't really prepared for it.

When you experience success, you can't just follow the same path and expect it to continue. You have to recognize that things will be different and the challenges you face as a team will change. Leadership requires you to understand the environment and adjust accordingly.

It's not like practices were a disaster. They just went past intense, to really tense. It felt different. Our guys were showing up to compete every day as they always did, and that was a good thing. It wasn't like we were feeling cocky because we beat a division I team. We knew we still hadn't won anything, so we still had a lot to prove. I remember putting a sign on our locker room door before our next practice after Iona that said "0-0." That was our record. Winning an exhibition game was not going to help us achieve our goal of winning a championship. We weren't cocky, we were tight.

We won our first three games of the season, but we didn't play great. We were tight and tense for most of the month of November, and I couldn't really figure it out. Like most issues, when you look back you see them more clearly. Had I known we were that uptight at the time I would have done something to change it, but as a young head coach I couldn't see it. I just thought I was driving my team to compete at a championship level, and I conflated tension with intensity.

Our fourth game was at home against Keene State, our first league game being against our biggest rival. And they came into Providence and beat us. They were a great team that year—they would go on to the Sweet 16 (more on that later). They were better that day, from

89

tap to buzzer. They controlled us pretty well, and we sat in our locker room after the game at 3-1, wondering what was wrong. We competed at a fine level, but Keene was the tougher team. And as I always said to my players, the tougher team wins. The tougher team had won at Iona, and the tougher team had won that day in our gym.

I've never been a big believer that you have to lose first to learn how to win, and I'd much rather learn from a bad win than a tough loss. But that early loss to Keene was important to us. It's not like I all of the sudden figured out what was wrong. But that early loss just allowed us to take a deep breath. It broke some of the tension. Without knowing it, we had felt like we were supposed to be perfect. If we can beat a division I team we should have no trouble running the table against a division III schedule. But it obviously wasn't going to be that easy. And now we realized we weren't going to be undefeated.

It wasn't like that Keene loss knocked us off our pedestal. We hadn't gotten overconfident because of the Iona win. It actually confirmed that what we felt was true—something wasn't right. Losing that game to Keene allowed us to go back to being just another good division III team that had to prepare to win on every night. It eased the tension and allowed us to reset our mentality.

Trust Is Essential

After the Keene loss we continued to practice hard and improve, with a lot less tension. We got back on the winning track, winning our next three games including a double-OT league win at Plymouth State—a really important win to avoid starting 0-2 in league play. At 6-1 in December, we went to the Coast Guard Academy to play a non-league game. It was another game that would have a big impact on my development as a leader.

We showed up at Coast Guard having won three in a row and we were just awful. We were a better team than they were, and I really didn't feel like we took them lightly. We just couldn't do anything right. We'd execute perfectly and we'd drop the ball out of bounds. We'd make the right pass ahead and we'd miss the layup. It was one of those nights where we were trying, but we were just completely out of sync.

I called three timeouts in the first half. The first one I was trying to shake my team up a little bit and get them going. That didn't really work, so the second one I tried to settle them down. Relax, we have a long way to go, let's get back to being ourselves. But that didn't work either. As Coast Guard continued to build their lead and half-time approached, I didn't really know what to do. We had a fast-break opportunity after finally getting a stop and my point guard dribbled the ball off of his foot. I called my third time out.

I felt at that point I needed to show my team I really trusted them. I believed in what we were doing in practice every day, and I knew we were committed to each other. We had taken a great approach every day. The team I saw on the floor at Coast Guard was unrecognizable. Everybody felt awful about the way we were playing, so the last thing they needed was for me to add more negative emotion to the situation. I went with a different approach.

What They Need Vs. What You Feel

We were down 19 with about 5:00 to go in the first half when I called that third timeout. The guys came over to the huddle, and I just laughed. I couldn't help it. I said "Wow, guys, what did you eat before the game today. We look like we're playing with a football out there. Is everyone okay?" I was literally laughing in disbelief at how bad we were playing. I wasn't really sure what to do, but I knew adding more tension to the situation wouldn't help. I wanted them to laugh at themselves. I thought back to practice and said, "Look, I know who we are, and this isn't us. We are a lot better than this. I've seen it every day. So just promise me you'll keep competing for each other no matter what the score is, and I'm sure we'll get back to being ourselves." I didn't make any drastic changes or declarations. I just tried to re-center our team and get them to relax. I really trusted who we were every day, and I wanted them to do the same.

It was an essential lesson in leadership for me that day, and it really came out of necessity. I didn't know what to do, really, but I knew the team had earned my trust with their approach. What they needed in that moment was more important than what I felt, and my leadership needed to reflect that. It's easy to get that one backwards, with our emotion ruling the message. Watching my team get worked for 15 minutes wasn't a lot of fun, and I experienced a range of negative emotions. I wasn't feeling very good. But my team didn't need to know that. What they needed was something to help them get out of their funk. Something to break the tension, not add to it. They needed a reset, and a reminder that I believed in them.

Think about it when your team is struggling. You have to handle how you feel, and negative emotions in a bad situation are natural. But you have to lead based on what your team needs and put your own feelings aside. Leading with your emotions, while it might feel natural to you, is not productive. What your team needs is so much more important, and generally not tied to your emotions. It's one of the truly great challenges of leadership. Set aside how you are feeling and figure out what your team needs, and they will respond.

Finally, after that third timeout in the first half everything started getting back to normal. We started to play a lot looser while picking up the intensity a bit, and we chipped our way back into the game. We got back to being ourselves and got more comfortable. We finished the half with a flurry, and when we hit a three at the half-time buzzer it cut our deficit to seven.

At halftime our locker room felt like the winning one, even though we were down a touchdown. Our guys were feeling like themselves again. I just said, "Fellas, they made a huge mistake. They never put us away. This game is ours!" I wanted to feed off the positive emotion we had built.

We went out and played great in the second half, and Coast Guard put up a good fight. It was a great college basketball game. We won a close game in the final minute, one of the more satisfying results we had all year. And a win, because of how it happened, that I'll never forget.

The lesson that day was a great one. You want your players to trust you, but to get there you have to trust them. I trusted my team based on what I had seen us do every day, and 15 minutes of awful play wasn't going to change that. I knew that practice every day revealed our true character. I had to trust them.

When your team struggles, figure out what they need. Remove your emotion from the situation and focus on their true character. It's not about how you feel, it's about what they need. It is an incredibly challenging and essential balance to find as a leader.

A New Standard

We went into Christmas break at 8-1, having won five games in a row. The Keene State game was still our only loss. Due to the way the schedule worked, we would take close to three weeks off for finals and Christmas before getting back together in early January.

I was happy with where our team was over the break with just one loss, but the one loss was on my mind. To win our league, we'd have to get through Keene, and they were clearly tougher than us the first time we played. I decided over break that we had to raise the expectations for our team and develop a new level of toughness. We were good enough to win the league, but we were going to have to go through Keene to do it. They were tougher than us. That had to change.

When we came back in January, I put the new standard of toughness on the table for our guys. I asked them if they thought we could win the league, and they all said yes. I told them we had a plan to do just that, but we were going to have to change some things. The tone of our practices had to be a little different. I was going to hold them accountable for all of the toughness plays that needed to be made to be a championship team. They were all on board.

Keep Listening
January 2007

That January provided another great lesson in leadership for me, a reminder of the importance of listening.

As promised, when we came back to practice, I set a different tone. Practice was more intense. I was relentless with every toughness play and I had no let up. Our guys were coming back from a long break, so it was a little shocking for them. And I was fine with that. We needed to get tougher.

The problem was the extended break, combined with the new tone I was trying to set, led to some miserable practices. We were awful. The guys were out of playing shape after too many days off, and I kept driving them harder. I didn't have a lot of patience or let up, because I knew we had to be tougher. The combination didn't work, and for two days of practice everyone was miserable. I was convinced, however, that the new tone was something they needed to get used to.

After that second miserable practice, after the guys had gone home, I got a phone call in the office from Kinsey Durgin. Kinsey was unquestionably a team leader and also one of the best players in the league. His phone call turned out to be a very important conversation in my development as a head coach.

Kinsey started out by telling me how much he loved playing for me, and how everyone on the team felt the same way. He said the entire team was bought in to what we were doing, but for the last two days they noticed a different tone, and everyone was miserable.

"We all love playing for you. But the last two days haven't been the same. We feel like you are giving up on us, and you don't believe in us. We've had coaches give up on us before, and guys are afraid that is happening again. So, please don't give up on us."

I was taken aback. Kinsey and I had a great relationship, and the conversation was very cordial. But at first, I wasn't very comfortable. One of my players was basically calling me out as a coach and giving me constructive criticism. My first reaction was to defend myself. I was the head coach, right? Players don't tell the coach what to do. I was a little tense. Fortunately, I didn't get defensive.

We talked about why I was setting a different tone, because I didn't think we were tough enough. He agreed that we needed to get tougher, but he didn't think the guys were bought in to how we were going about it. The tougher tone was making everybody unhappy, and the tone was very negative. More importantly some of the guys were starting to turn on me and give up on the team. My approach was making us worse, not better.

I wasn't sure how to react. We had a good conversation, but I definitely felt like as the head coach my players shouldn't be telling me what to do. My ego was definitely bruised. I needed to figure out what to do. Luckily, I didn't respond in any way right on the phone, probably out of shock. Phil Jackson says, "When in doubt, do nothing," and luckily, I followed that advice. Because I didn't know what to do.

I called a friend of mine who was a veteran coach to have a conversation. I wanted to get another perspective and clear my mind to evaluate the conversation I just had with my captain. I needed to talk it out.

I explained to him what happened with the Kinsey phone call, and I'll never forget his reaction.

"You've got 'em."

I was surprised. "I've got 'em?"

"You've got 'em. If your senior captain felt comfortable enough to give you a call, to talk to you about what is going on in practice, and to tell you some things that the team thinks you need to do better – if he felt safe enough to have that conversation with you? You've got 'em. They are totally bought in. They are willing to lay it on the line for you. I'd listen to him, because he wouldn't be calling you if there wasn't some sort of issue."

That was an eye-opening way to look at it. If we had created a culture where the players were comfortable coming to me with things they felt needed to change, they had total belief in what we were doing. They trusted me and they trusted us – our culture – so much that they were willing to take a risk to fight for it. Wasn't that what I was always saying to them? It has to be worth fighting for, and Kinsey was fighting for it.

There had to be a level of safety in our program to have that kind of difficult conversation. There was no fear. That same level of safety allowed our players to lay it all on the line for one another every day, without concern for the result. And if they were telling me something was wrong, I needed to listen. The elite competitive environment we had created on the practice floor allowed Kinsey to call me and speak the truth.

Regardless of what the issue was, the fact that our culture was safe enough to have that conversation meant a lot. We had the team fully bought in, and I had to make sure I kept it that way. I spent the night thinking about that conversation and my approach, feeling better about the culture we were building.

The next day I spoke to the team about the conversation I had with Kinsey. I thanked him for calling me to talk, and I apologized for the tone that I had set in the first two practices after the break. I made it very clear that I would never give up on them. I again explained what I was doing and why I was doing it. I reiterated the point that we needed to get tougher to win the league, and the players agreed. I asked them how we were going to get there.

We came to an understanding that they would hold each other accountable for all of the toughness plays on a daily basis. I would make sure I pointed them out and coached them on it, but they would have to take responsibility. They needed to correct the behavior and make sure it was unacceptable. In return, I would make sure the tone stayed positive. I'd still coach them and hold them accountable, but I wouldn't get negative about it. They were going to take even more ownership. I had to give them the room.

To be honest, I wasn't entirely comfortable with it at first. I was glad we had the conversation, and it felt good to have my team back. The guys were much better in practice moving forward and competed at a high level. The atmosphere was positive and fun. But I still wasn't entirely sure that we'd be able to get tougher. I'd point out the soft plays in practice and I'd say "How are we going to change the behavior guys? How do you want to do it?" I tried not to yell or get too negative, and the point was more "you told me you were going to correct it, so what are we going to do about it?" It was risky as a coach, because I still didn't think we were tough enough. But it felt good to get my team back. And little did I know we were creating more trust and ownership.

This was probably the most significant experience I had where I truly understood the value of listening to my players. And my belief in that has only grown over my career. I can watch practice, evaluate film, and talk to my staff as much as I want. I always learn the most about my team when I listen to my players. I try to talk to my players as much as possible. There is no better way to understand the pulse of your team.

Kinsey called me and challenged me, the first time that happened to me as a head coach. He went about it the right way, with a measured, respectful tone, but I still was caught off guard. My first instinct was to fight back and establish the fact that I was in charge. I'm glad I didn't do that. That conversation really helped me grow as a leader. It gave me an understanding of the value of a safe culture, and how important it was for me to listen. I had created an atmosphere where my players wanted to take ownership, and I had to allow them to do that. It felt really uncomfortable at first, but it was a big step in forming our championship culture.

The Lesson They Receive

One other important leadership lesson I reinforced that week was that the message you deliver isn't nearly as important as the message your team receives. I had explained clearly to our group what we were going to do that January, and they were on board with it. I gave them the why. But when I got to executing the plan, the message they were receiving was very different from the one I was trying to deliver. I thought I was showing them we needed to be tougher. They thought I no longer believed in them, that I was giving up on them.

It didn't matter what message I thought I was delivering because it wasn't getting across that way. What really matters is the message they are receiving, no matter what you think you are saying to them. That responsibility falls not on your team, but on you as the leader.

Short-Term Goals

We didn't play great right out of the gate in January, but we played well enough to win. As I mentioned January can be hard at the D3 level because the calendar forced us to take almost 20 days off. I learned to evaluate my team based on where we were at that time, versus where we hoped to be. I wanted to win the league, I knew we were good enough and that was our goal – but no team is good enough to win their league in January. And the good news is you don't have to. We were still learning and growing as a team, but we were winning games while we were doing it. The original standard I was using to evaluate was not about how we played or whether we won or lost, it was whether or not we played well enough to win the league. And that was a mistake. We didn't have to win the league in January. We needed to handle what was in front of us and keep getting better. The pressure to win the league in January could para-lyze us, and I had to get away from that.

I was looking too far ahead, and I was worried that our team was doing the same. It's great to have long-term goals, but day-to-day to get the most out of your team, you have to think short-term as well. We talked so much about winning the league that we forgot about enjoying the process every day. I changed that. We started to talk about our short-term goals as a group.

Get better today, win our next game. That became our approach. I wanted us to focus entirely on today and nothing else. But I also felt like we needed to celebrate success, and the result did matter. My expectations about playing like a championship team every night were unrealistic. Success is hard. Finding a way to win every night, while not playing great but still getting better – that, in fact, was playing like a championship team.

What I didn't really appreciate at the time, but I do recognize looking back, is the way we were playing defensively. We had estab-lished ourselves as the best defensive team in the league, and even though we weren't always in a great flow offensively, we were usually pretty hard to score on. We really guarded you, and that is what made us different. That is where we started in our first meeting, when we talked about winning the league. On the defensive side. And we were doing it. It was starting to separate us, just as we had discussed.

Another Setback

We continued to improve in early January and kept getting the right results, although I didn't feel we were clicking on offense. We won our first six games after the break, running our winning streak to 11 in a row since the Keene loss. We were 14-1 and off to the best start in school history. As much as we tried to celebrate the day to day success, it still felt a little bit like we were doing what we were supposed to. We expected to win. Did that come from the Iona game, and getting off to a 14-1 start? Absolutely. Nothing creates a winning environment like winning. But it was also about the investment in what we were doing every day. Our guys believed in the way we were practicing, the way we were getting better, and what it meant to our growth as a team. We were creating something special, and, luckily, I started to realize that in January and made sure I'd remind my team of that regularly.

I still didn't feel entirely comfortable with how tough we were as a team, but we were practicing hard, defending well and winning games. I knew we were getting better, but we still had room to improve. We hadn't clicked yet. And we had a great test in front of us.

At 14-1, we went up to Keene State in late January for the rematch of the only game we had lost all year. It was obviously a huge game as they were atop the league and had already gotten us at home. We knew what getting swept by them would likely mean – it was their league.

We were focused and prepared, and we went up to Keene and played well. But they were better than us. It was a big game between two great teams, but they made the winning plays. They got us again.

I turned to my assistant, Matt O'Brien, on the bus heading home and said simply, "We just aren't tough enough. They are just better than us." He agreed. It was the truth. Keene was really good and might have been as talented or more talented than we were. But they were also physically really tough. They played hard just like we did, but there was an edge to the way they competed that we had trouble matching. There was that toughness thing that I had worried about. We still hadn't solved it – at least not well enough to beat Keene,

We returned to Providence and had to face reality. Keene had beaten us twice and they were a game ahead of us, essentially giving them a one and a half game lead for the league title with seven league games remaining. We weren't crushed by the loss, and that might have been a good thing. I give my team a lot of credit for that mentality. It was when I first started to think about our relationship with losing. That second loss to Keene didn't deflate us.

We realized Keene was really good, and we were in unchartered territory. I wish I could say I came up with a magical approach after we lost to Keene a second time to rally the crew, but I really had nothing. We were 14-2 and having the best year in the history of the school, but we were also faced with the reality of having lost twice in our league to our biggest rival.

We accomplished a lot in my nine years at RIC, but there was one accomplishment I was always very proud of that went a little unnoticed – that Keene team was the only team that ever swept us. We had eight teams in our league, so that's 63 home and home opportunities over nine years. You hate getting swept as a coach and responding to beat a team that already beat you says a lot about your mental toughness. That Keene team was the only team in our league to beat us twice over nine seasons, and we weren't done with them.

It was an odd place to be mentally. Ultimately, this team would teach me about the value of disconnecting the work from the results, and how that leads to success. At the time, I wasn't really thinking that way. Luckily for me we had a mature group that had been through a lot together, and that made us mentally tough.

The only approach I came up with was to remind everyone that the final chapter had not been written. It was late January and we had eight games left to play, with seven in our league. We just went back to work.

Relationship with Losing

After that second loss to Keene I started thinking about our relationship with losing. It wasn't a philosophy I developed as much as one I was forced to deal with. Our goal was to win our league but we got swept by our rival, so we had to find a different approach. I made sure not to focus on Keene or winning the league anymore, instead turning the approach to getting better every day and winning our next game. It was all process, with an understanding that the results did matter. What we were doing every day said everything about who we were, and that would put us in a position to find success.

You hear the phrase often that we are "in a results-based business." But who isn't? Who is in a business where the results don't matter? They do matter, and that is okay. But the question is how do you get the best results? And I'm convinced it is by separating yourself from those results and focusing completely on what you can control – the process.

Jim Steen was the long time men's and women's swimming coach at Kenyon, and he won more national titles than any coach of any college sport at any level. He had a great quote for his teams that I recited often.

"Find a place within yourselves where success and failure do not matter, where you can compete without compromise."

I love what that quote represents, and I think it's how you develop the competitive edge needed for elite success. Separate from the results. We talked about how results were how everyone else was going to judge us – by our record – but that was never how we would judge ourselves. We would judge ourselves on what we did every day. It was very challenging in a business where the scoreboard was public. But we committed to it.

The emphasis we put on the process went a long way towards how we dealt with failure. It never really seemed to affect us moving forward. We had great competitors who cared about winning and absolutely hated to lose, no doubt about it. But the next day after a tough loss, when my stomach was tied in knots, the players were usually over it. When we lost that second game to Keene I was amazed how resilient and positive the players were. There was no one hanging their heads or feeling sorry for themselves. They were moving forward, and they brought me along with them.

Part of this was all 19-year-olds think they are superheroes and don't let anything phase them. But our relentless focus on the process and the approach our players took went a long way towards avoiding those hangovers that many teams had after losing games. We didn't take our wins or our losses too seriously, because what was important was what we were doing today. We never really let anything snowball.

Losing is something every organization has to deal with. It's a hard balance to find. Losing stings, and you never want to accept it. But you have to make sure it doesn't impact you moving forward. Separating our team from the result as much as possible was a huge part of our championship culture.

Elite teams and elite competitors have a great relationship with failure, as odd as that may sound. It doesn't mean they accept it or losing doesn't bother them. Great competitors hate to lose. But they know how to handle it, how to process it, and how to move forward. My team in our second year taught me that lesson. We knew we were really good, we believed in the way we competed every day, and losing was not going to get in our way. It was a sign we were mentally tough. It's not an easy place to find.

Your team will have a lot more success if you develop the correct relationship with failure. It comes down to two important aspects of your culture – belief and perspective. A strong belief in what you are doing every day is essential—the bedrock your team can always count on. The right perspective keeps you grounded in the process, win or lose. You show up with the same approach, regardless. Elite teams that experience consistent winning know how to handle defeat.

Another Setback
February 2007

Our approach was important, because we would lose again in another 10 days when Amherst came to town. We won two league games after the loss at Keene, and then we faced Amherst at home, who was the number one team in the country. It was a huge game at our place and a great test for us. Their coach, Dave Hixon, had reached out in the off-season to see if we wanted to play, and they were projected to be the number one team in the country at that point. I jumped at the chance for a number of reasons – I wanted our program to be associated with the elite teams, and I also knew we were going to be pretty good. But the main reason I wanted to play the best teams was the same reason we played Iona—I knew it would force us to prepare at a high level. Challenging my team was important, and I knew we'd learn a lot about ourselves that night.

We were no match for Amherst. They were really talented, big, and physical, and we just couldn't score. We competed really hard, but they just shut us down, holding us to 48 points and beating us by 14. It was our second loss in our last four games, and our third loss of the year. But it was a little different. They handled us pretty easily. It was really the only game we played all year where we couldn't get anything going. They took us out of the game right away and controlled us all night.

We were disappointed with the loss, but not crushed, and this is where I again took a cue from my players on how to handle defeat. There was a lot of hype surrounding the game locally and a great crowd, with local television stations on hand. Our guys were pumped to play, and obviously down about losing. But we had developed this rare balance of confidence and humility that was essential to our core. We showed up every day expecting to beat you, and willing to accept nothing else. But when we didn't get it done, we were able to admit that the other team was just better than us and get back to work. Amherst was better than us, and that was okay. It wasn't going to affect who we were every day. It was an incredibly mature perspective for a team to have, and it taught me a lot about dealing with failure. It's a tricky relationship, for sure, because you never want to get used to it. But our guys were in good spirits the next day at practice, and as usual they brought me back to the right frame of mind.

At that point we were 16-3 with five league games left. We'd also gotten some good news a few days before we played Amherst in that Keene had actually lost again, so we were tied for first place. While no one thought that Keene would lose again, a regular season league title would still be the first in school history, so we got a little juice from being in first place. We stayed focused on our routine—getting better, winning our next game. But I'm sure we all thought about winning our last five games and at least sharing a league title.

Playing for Each Other

We were oddly in a really good place having lost two of our last four games after starting out 14-1. We were actually in a better place mentally than we were when we beat Iona, and I owe that to the six seniors on our team. They had been through a lot together in four years and now seemed to be enjoying the ride. They had let go of the results, and they simply didn't want to let their teammates down. We weren't playing to win. We were playing for each other.

Another lesson my team taught me that year: Teams that learned to play for one another were really hard to beat. Everything we were competing for that year went from external (our record) to internal (each other). Strangely enough, we probably felt more pressure internally to perform, but it made us a lot looser. It belonged to us. It didn't matter what everyone else thought. We were bought in to what we were doing, and that was plenty good enough for everyone in our gym.

How did we get there? It was a combination of things – the maturity of the six seniors and what they had been through, our focus on the process over results, and our dedicated belief in how we went about our business every day. What we were doing was really tough, but we loved it. And what we loved about it was sharing it with one another. I really believe the bond our seniors had, mostly established before I arrived, became the glue of our championship culture. It was crucial to them to be able to look one another in the eye and know they'd given each other everything they had.

Create an environment within your organization where your team refuses to let one another down. Emphasize that what you are doing is for each other, to satisfy your internal standards. Put your team in positions where they have to count on each other. They may believe in you and what you are doing, but the energy they find for each other is really important. That is the strength I felt with this team. It was a very powerful competitive edge.

Our next game was against Eastern Connecticut at home on the first Saturday in February, and we got the job done. It wasn't a dominant performance, but we were tough enough and we were ready to play. We weren't really score-checking the rest of the league because it wasn't really our focus. We left the gym 17-3 with four games left to play.

I saw Kinsey as I was leaving the building after that game. He was walking to his car just in front of me, and he turned and casually said, "Hey Coach, did you see Keene lost?" I hadn't even looked. No one was really thinking that way. It honestly wasn't on my mind. But UMass-Boston had beaten Keene State. I took it in stride, I didn't want to react in front of Kinsey like it was that big of a deal. We weren't focused on Keene, we weren't even talking about them. But, obviously, it was a big deal. I got in my car and took a deep breath. Our season had reset right back to where we were after we beat Iona and started this journey. We had completely forgotten about winning the league, and once we did, it turned out we were the team to beat. We had four games left and to win them all meant the first outright league title in school history.

The Noise

It's interesting how things you can't control can change the mentality of your team throughout the course of a season. It's one reason the mental side of the game is so important. Many things will affect your team's mentality and in turn affect their ability to perform. You need to constantly have a pulse on it and understand how to coach it. We felt a ton of pressure after winning an exhibition game in November, and it no doubt affected our ability to prepare. Then Keene pops us and we had to reset. I tried to make our team tougher over the break and it backfired, but we found ways to win. In late January, Keene gets us again and we had to face the reality that our main goal—to win the league—was likely unrealistic. Another mental reset. Two weeks later, including a loss to Amherst, we were in the driver's seat – because of a result that we had nothing to do with. Dealing with the mental side is a critical element of the journey.

I knew my challenge was to keep my team levelheaded. All of the noise around our program could affect the way we showed up every day. I'm not a believer in the "Just stay focused" or "Block out the noise" approach to leadership. I feel like that's almost a cop-out, a way to shun the responsibility. I wanted to recognize the noise and deal with it.

After we beat Iona, we didn't really do a good job with that. And we were really tight and showed up with unrealistic expectations every day. After we lost to Keene (both times), we addressed it. How do we feel right now? How are we going to respond to this? It was very important with regards to our approach. When we lost to Amherst, we kind of knew who we were and how to react at that point—because we had lost twice to Keene. We were more comfortable, but we still had to deal with it.

If you are capable of simply ignoring the noise, you are better at this than me. Recognize the noise. Talk about it. Discuss it with your team. I understand the approach that you don't want to make too big of a deal out of it by paying attention to it. But in my experience, the noise becomes a bigger deal when you don't address it. A great friend of mine and the CEO of York Consulting, LLC, Phil O'Brien, whose son Matt was my assistant coach, always says, "See reality for what it is, and act accordingly." The noise around your program is reality. Act accordingly. Ignore it at your own peril.

So now we controlled the league and history was in our own hands. Our focus on the process really made a big difference—not to mention the maturity of our seniors. Our guys knew we were four wins away from winning the league. We talked about it. We didn't avoid it. I wanted them to think about it. I was thinking about it! We acknowledged the opportunity to do something special, and we talked about how to handle it.

Pressure

Coaching that team, in that moment, when we realized we controlled our own narrative to win the league, was one of the great joys of my coaching life. We had great kids, we were really talented, and they had bought in to an approach that was uncommon. They gave me the greatest gift a young leader can receive – they believed in me. We had so much fun competing together every day. You could literally feel the trust and belief we had for one another.

It's also the most pressure I have ever felt as a coach. To be truthful, it was kind of startling at first. I never thought I would feel that way. I've always been pretty good at staying composed, keeping things in perspective and separating from the result. A bad practice always bothered me more than a tough loss, because we had a lot more control over a practice. I never let the wins or losses get to me, so any pressure I felt was all about how we operated at practice day to day.

But the second half of that year was different. First of all, we were trying to do something that had never been done before. Second, we had six seniors who were on their third coach and had been through so much together. They were GREAT kids who believed in me from the beginning, despite things being completely different. And of course, the pressure to win is real. It's fun. We had a lot of local hype surrounding our program, and we were enjoying it. Everyone on campus was talking to us, the crowds were great, the local news was in our gym just about every day. But the biggest thing for me was I thought the kids deserved the recognition. There was a big difference between being a great team that had a great run and won a lot of big games, and one that won a championship and hung a banner. Banners fly forever. The legacy of those players was on the line, and I felt a ton of pressure to deliver for them. I had to learn to handle it.

Handling pressure is a different beast in any arena, but something high performing teams always have to deal with. I prefer to embrace it, to talk about it with the players and understand how it feels. I don't think it makes the situation bigger by talking about it; I think it allows you to manage it. Let's talk about how we feel and what impact it may have on us. And then we'll work on handling it. Pressure is a privilege in my mind, it's a sign that you are in the right place. It's not something to run away from. I talked to my guys about how they felt, and told them how I felt as well, saying, "We've earned that feeling, fellas." We earned the right to have that level of energy, anxiety and intensity every day when we woke up. As a great competitor, it's what you live for. Talking about it established that it was okay to feel nerves and anxiety—not just for them, but for myself as well.

You have to be intentional about handling pressure. Don't just talk about it. I wanted that level of intensity and pressure in our practices every day, because I knew we would feel it in the games. But we also wanted to separate from it at times. We took our guys out to fun meals to watch a game when we could. I remember going to movies by myself during that stretch, just to shut everything off. We'd make sure we laughed during film sessions or cracked jokes in practice to lighten the mood. We embraced the pressure, planned for it, but then found some ways to separate from it. We wanted that pressure on us, but I don't think anyone wants to feel it all of the time. We tried to normalize pressure by dealing with it.

Doubling Down on Confidence

We continued to play well. Three of our last four games were on the road, and we picked up wins at Western Connecticut, at Plymouth State, and at home against UMass-Dartmouth, all by double figures. We were confident and comfortable, and all of a sudden, one game away from winning a title. We would finish the season on the road against UMass-Boston, a team that was in the bottom half of the league (but ironically the last team to beat Keene State).

That last week it was harder to control the noise. Now it was right in front of us, just 40 minutes away. There was so much energy in the gym that week getting ready for the game, and there was no way to fight it. We had to find a way to make that energy a positive and to keep our composure. I cut practices shorter than I normally did because of the way we were flying around. I felt we were ready, and I wanted to respect the energy our guys were giving. I knew that Saturday would be emotional.

The ride up to Boston was exciting. It was nervous energy combined with the confidence and trust that we had developed throughout the year. It was a special feeling.

We came out at UMass-Boston flying. We were a significantly better team and we played like it, our confidence and toughness on full display. We had a double-digit lead at halftime, but we knew UMass-Boston had the talent and athleticism to come back and beat us. I'm sure a few guys thought back to the semi-final game from a year ago. Our job was far from done.

Finding the right level of confidence while also staying grounded was my challenge at that point. We were playing great and we knew we were better. I wanted to ride that energy. But I also knew that over-confidence was really the only way UMass Boston could get back in the game. I had to trust what I knew about my team. Your team might not be able to handle success, and you need to keep a fire lit under them at all times. Other teams might feel great about the confidence you give them knowing you believe in them, and you want them to see that. The best way to push the right buttons with your team is to get to know them really well and trust them.

I did something different that halftime, something I've rarely done as a coach. I went the full confidence route, bordering on arrogance. I trusted my team completely. They knew what was at stake, and they were handling it. We had never been in that situation before, and I didn't want our guys thinking about hanging on for a win. I wanted to stay aggressive.

Coaching with a big lead is a lot more uncomfortable than you would think. A lot of coaches will talk about the inevitable run the other team is going to make, but I didn't want to make that a reality – or even a possibility. After we talked about some minor basketball stuff we might have to face (more pressure, faster pace), I took the leap. I said, "I want to bury this team. We came here to win the league, and they are in the way. They aren't in our class. I don't want them for a minute to think they can play with us. I want to blow them out."

My team was hungry, and I wanted to feed them confidence. If you believe your team is mature enough to handle it, continue to give them confidence. A combination of confidence and maturity can be very powerful, and luckily for me, my team had both.

We came out of the locker room after halftime and continued to play with great energy, playing hard and together. We kept making plays, and when UMass-Boston did go on a run we handled it with composure. We controlled the entire game. The lead never got to single digits and we ended up winning by 18 points – capturing RIC's first ever Little East Conference Championship.

There aren't too many better feelings for a coach than the bus ride home after winning the league. There was this tremendous combination of accomplishment, joy and satisfaction, with a little relief mixed in for the head coach. Championship teams walk together forever, and this would be the first RIC team do so. The t-shirts we wore as a team when I first took over said, "Win the League" on them, and in Boston, that day, we had done just that.

Success Is Never Final

Once again, the mental dynamic for our team had changed. We were now champions. It had only been four weeks since we left Keene State with our second league loss, and winning the league wasn't even in the conversation. But we had reset our mentality, kept improving, and now we were on top.

We were also in unchartered territory. None of us had ever done this before. I told our guys, when we got back to campus, to celebrate what we had done and enjoy it. I didn't want them to think about next week, I wanted them to think about being champions. We would take Sunday off, but on Sunday I wanted them to start thinking about change. About what would be different. When we went to class on Monday we'd be showing up as champions for the first time, and that would be a different feeling. Everything around our program would feel different, and we'd have to deal with that. Things have changed, let's make sure we are ready to handle it.

I thought about how to handle this level of success. We spend a lot of time in coaching and leadership thinking about failure, but not as much on success. Failure has a pretty routine script to follow—work harder, stay together, put in more time, etc. You know things have to change. But success changes the dynamic around you, as we learned throughout the year. And this was more than just one game, this was hang-a-banner success. Again, we needed a plan to handle it.

The post-season comes at you pretty fast, so there isn't a lot of time to get prepared. We won the league on a Saturday, and the first game of the post-season was on Tuesday, so with a day off on Sunday, we only had one day to practice.

Fortunately, we had already developed an intentional approach to handling success. We had developed great habits and I was very comfortable those would continue. I knew our guys were feeling great and I wanted them to feel that way. I wanted us to expect to win and carry the confidence of a championship team. But I also knew we were probably feeling a little too good about ourselves, and it might affect our approach to practice. It was natural considering what we had accomplished. We all just had to be aware of it.

Once again, we had to be ready to adjust, despite our success. You can't just stay comfortable and ride it out. We needed to address what we were feeling and think about how it might affect our approach. I needed to assess our feelings, our mood and our actions. We talked about how we felt and how it might impact us.

Elite success doesn't continue by chance. Put an intentional approach in place for your organization to adjust to it and you'll stay ahead of the curve.

EIGHT

LEADERSHIP EVOLVES

MARCH 2007

We were in a different situation now as a team, so we needed an adjusted approach. For us to keep winning, we had to get better. The post-season was win or go home, and we had to prepare for that.

The Little East Tournament started on that Tuesday with each of the top four seeds hosting a quarterfinal game in their own gym. We would play the eighth seed, Southern Maine, at home to start the tournament. After Tuesday, the highest remaining seed then hosted the final four on Friday and Saturday.

I took a practical approach. I thought I needed to bring our team back to reality, to get them to understand that what we had done in the past didn't matter much anymore. The reality was winning the league only bought us 40 minutes at home. That was it. We hadn't earned the right to host the tournament; we would host one game against the eighth seed. If we lost, it was over. Those 40 minutes at home were the only reward we got for winning the league.

That helped us get back to reality and focus only on the game in front of us. I also started to think about the emotion of the post-season. How it would feel different. There was a new emotion that we were going to have to face in the tournament – desperation. Every team playing knows (for the most part) that if they lose, their season is over. That type of desperation is powerful and an emotion you don't deal with much during the year.

Leadership and Change

In the regular season, even later in the year when the pecking order is somewhat established in your league, teams are still trying to play to their personality. It's hard for a coach to significantly change how they are going to play game to game based on their opponent. But in the post-season, everything changes. A team's personality and how they want to play is no longer relevant. It's a one game season. If playing a matchup zone gives them the best chance to win, they are going to do it. If it means their more talented players need to break off plays and try and create to win, they'll do it. Desperation is a dangerous and potentially effective emotion for bad teams in the post-season. We had to be ready for that. I made sure to tell my guys to expect a different Southern Maine team than we had seen during the regular season. Expect the unexpected.

Leadership is about change. It's assessing the reality of your situation and adapting to it. And it's constant. Leadership is fluid and highly contextual. What is going on in and around your organization dictates the necessary leadership. Leadership is rarely, if ever, maintaining the status quo. This holds true no matter how much success you are having. The environment around your organization is changing and your job is to prepare your team for it.

Less Control

I wanted to guard against being tight in the post-season. I knew it would feel different for our guys. But I wanted the confidence that we had earned to carry the day. Expect change, but know we are prepared to handle it. Teams that get nervous, that start to worry about the result, they get beat. We tried to coach confidence with our guys all year, and we needed to do it in the post-season as well.

I kept using the term "Scared goes home" in the post-season. Don't worry about making mistakes. Take a chance. Take a risk. Make a play. I told them to make more mistakes than Southern Maine—because that meant we weren't afraid. Go for a steal. Pull-up for three in transition. Throw a dime to your teammate. I kept telling them I wanted playmakers in the post-season.

I was trying to establish the right mentality, one that would allow us to handle the success we were experiencing. I wanted to avoid any thinking that would make them tight. I learned that the less control I had over my team in big games, the better we played, and it started with that first championship team.

When your team is in a big spot, trust your preparation and give up control. That may seem hard to do, but it's how you get the most out of your personnel. We had won the league for a reason—because we had talent and we knew how to execute together. I wanted to avoid taking control in the post-season. I wanted my team to have more confidence and more freedom to do the job. I wasn't moving chess pieces around. I wanted to turn them loose.

Over our nine years at Rhode Island College, our approach to the post-season was very successful. We went 21-3 in the Little East Tournament, and we would play in eight straight championship games, winning six of them. We went 11-8 in the NCAA tournament and finished overall 34-12 in the post-season, a winning percentage of 74%.

Plan B

One great challenge as a leader in a big spot is you have to buy-in to what you are selling to your team. It's easy to feel like your team is prepared and things will go smoothly. You want to have that confidence in them. But you still need to be prepared if things don't go your way. You have to have a plan B. Finding that balance is difficult.

I learned that lesson in my first post-season game as the top seed. We ended up in a dogfight with Southern Maine. They were not very talented, but they were very deliberate and well coached, and they would always play the game to attack our weaknesses. They knew we wanted to play fast, so they would play extra slow, trying to limit possessions. They didn't have any thoughts about style of play, all they wanted to do was make it hard for us. There was a lot of desperation in their mentality—in a good way.

I was confident we were in the right mindset approaching the game, and I don't really remember our guys feeling tight. But as the game wore on and it stayed close, the pressure definitely got to us. And that's where my mentality could have been better. I was more in disbelief that we were struggling against them, instead of expecting it just like I had told my team. I realized a few minutes into the game that I needed to do everything I could to keep our guys loose, but we were on the brink of getting upset and our guys knew it. We couldn't make shots and we couldn't get the game going at our pace. Southern Maine was slowing us down, and they kept us from finding a good rhythm.

I once heard the great hall-of-fame coach, Bob Hurley, talk about the best teams he ever coached, and what made them so great. One of the things he said was his best teams could always beat you in different ways. If you wanted to play the game fast, they'd beat you in the 90s. But if you wanted to play slow, they could play at a methodical pace and still beat you. They could beat you however they needed to, but they were going to beat you. And that is a great lesson to learn for high performing teams.

You always need to have a different plan ready to win. No matter what your "big game" is, make sure you have a plan B. You know exactly how you expect things to go, and if they follow that path, you'll have no problems. But you might have to find a different way. Is your team prepared to succeed in multiple ways? You want them to be comfortable when things get uncomfortable, which they inevitably will – especially if you are the top seed and expected to win! You may have a core approach to success that you don't want to deviate from, which is fine. But when the unexpected comes your way, your team will look to you for an answer. Make sure you are prepared. In our first post-season game in 2007, I'm not sure I was.

We battled with Southern Maine down to the wire, and the game went into overtime. We pulled it out when Brian Stanko, one of the four seniors on that team who came off the bench, buried a big three-pointer with the clock running down and the game tied late in OT. We didn't win the game as much as we survived. We beat the eight seed at the horn. I'm not sure I fully prepared my team to win that game at the pace it was played at, because I didn't really expect it. I was expecting us to play well. We did just enough to move on and host the league tournament that weekend.

When Success Doesn't Feel Right

I knew the next day I had a challenge on my hands. We had barely survived and none of us felt good about it. Now we had two days to get ready to play in the semi-finals on Friday night. Everyone in the program (myself included) had a bad feeling about the Southern Maine game, and people were calling and texting asking me "what happened?" Luckily, I got sick of it and finally just changed my mindset. We won a conference tournament game as the top seed for the first time ever, and now we were hosting the semifinals on Friday. That was the truth. I got a little pissed about it, and that changed my mentality. But my players couldn't shake it. When I saw a couple of them during the day, they asked me if I had watched the film, and wondered aloud, "How bad was it?"

I knew I needed to change the mentality of my team. It was an odd place to be, handling success that didn't feel right. I could convince myself to start fresh on that Wednesday. We were the top seed hosting the league semi-finals for the first time in school history. We'd have given anything to be in that position at the beginning of the year. But how we got there – by barely getting past Southern

Maine—was hard to ignore. I needed a way to get the players mentally past what happened the night before and get locked in for the semi-finals. But I couldn't just say, "Hey, we got it done, time to move on." It was handling a different kind of success, the kind that didn't feel right.

Then I checked my email.

I had gotten to know Stan Van Gundy through a good friend of mine from high school. He had worked with Stan on the radio in Florida when Stan was with the Miami Heat. Stan had just recently stepped down as the head coach of the Heat, and as a true basketball junkie when Stan had time, he would watch our games online.

Stan happened to be watching our game against Southern Maine and sent me an email afterwards. He congratulated us on the win and said he learned in the NBA that, especially when it came to the playoffs, the result was the only thing that mattered. How you got there was irrelevant. He then went on to comment about how good of a job he thought we did in certain areas – defending, rebounding the ball, and not turning the ball over – when we were struggling to score. He remarked how doing those things when we couldn't score was the sign of a championship team. He also said we had a very clear identity as a team—tough half-court defense, unselfish on offense—and that when he could tell a team's identity after watching just a few games, it was a sign the team was both well coached and fully committed to one another. He was very positive about what he saw in our team.

It was also exactly what I needed. I knew exactly how to knock my team out of our little funk.

When I got to our meeting room before practice, I told the guys that a friend of mine had watched the game and sent me some comments, and I wanted to share them with the team. I went through the entire email, emphasizing Stan's points about how well we had played considering we couldn't score. I finished it with

"Good luck this weekend. My daughter has a swim meet on Friday but if I get home in time, I'll be watching. Stan Van Gundy."

When the guys heard that name, their jaws just about hit the floor. They had no idea who I was reading a note from, and the fact that an NBA coach was watching them play blew them away. Not to mention, his analysis was that we should feel really good about the way we played. I could tell by the look on their faces that things had changed. The hangover was gone. I had gotten lucky and found something that could instantly snap them out of it.

Immediately, we stopped feeling sorry for ourselves. I emphasized three keys to winning before every game – defend the ball, rebound the ball, and take care of the ball. And we had done all three. We felt bad because Southern Maine was able to slow down the game and we struggled to score. But we won the game because we executed our three keys to winning. We should feel good about that. Especially when we couldn't score! We walked out of that room and into practice feeling good about ourselves, with Southern Maine behind us and the league championship in our sights.

Almost immediately our guys were back in a good mental space – probably because I was as well. We were facing a good UMass-Dartmouth team on Friday in the semi-finals, a game we all knew would not be easy. We reiterated our post-season mentality to our guys for two days because I didn't want them getting tight after the scare against Southern Maine. I wanted playmakers out on the floor. Scared goes home. We were back to being ourselves in practice leading up to that Friday night.

Get Their Mind Right

We were matched up against a good UMass-Dartmouth team in the semi-final that had finished fourth in the league, but we had already beaten them twice. This presented another challenge for the mentality of our team. Have you ever heard the theory that it's hard to beat the same team three times? My guess is you have, because you hear it around sports—especially football and basketball – all of the time. Coaches, players analysts all say it—it's hard to beat a team three times.

The only problem with the theory is that it's not actually true.

I've always felt comfortable challenging conventional thinking, and as I've made my way through my coaching career, I've discovered that college basketball has plenty of conventional thinking. So much of what we do and say comes from the fact that other coaches have done and said them. We don't take the time to understand—or question—why we do them. Is this the same in your business? Don't blindly accept the way everyone operates as the right approach for your team. Challenge the preconceived notions about how to find success. I'm sure you'll find some different approaches that help you.

After our win over Southern Maine, chatter around our program was about how it was hard to beat a team three times. Since we had swept seven of the eight teams in our league, we were going to have to beat a team three times at least twice to win the tournament. I didn't want our guys thinking it was going to be hard, because I didn't really believe it. If we beat them twice already, we are probably the better team. Didn't we want to be in that situation?

I read some data online from a study that was done over a 10-year period in college basketball that tracked the third meeting between two schools, where the same team had won the first two games. The study showed that 73% of the time, the team that won the first two meetings also won the third matchup. Almost three out of four! Yet, we still heard consistently how hard it was to beat a team three times. It didn't seem that hard to me.

After the OT win over Southern Maine, it became more ingrained in our mentality, as if a hard earned win proved the theory that beating a team three times was really hard. The first thing I told my team was we didn't have to beat UMass-Dartmouth three times, we only had to beat them once. The second thing I told them was the reason we had beaten them twice was because we were the better team. In the third matchup, would you rather be the better team, or not? I wanted to be on the better team.

Again, don't shy away from the mentality of your team. Don't fall into the trap of overlooking it. Coach it. And don't be afraid to challenge conventional thinking. You'll discover ways to help your team you may not otherwise have thought about. A team that is mentally in the right place is free to give you their best effort.

Illusory Truth

The illusory truth effect is something leaders have to be aware of, and certainly something I see a lot of in coaching. It comes from a study done at Villanova and Temple in the 1970s, where scientists discovered that people would believe false information after they are continually exposed to it. The research says that familiarity has a significant impact on whether or not we think something is true.

The more we hear something, regardless of whether it is true or not, the more we believe it. Think about that for a minute. Regardless of whether something is true or not, if you continue to hear it you will start to believe it. This can have a significant impact on your team. Information is very powerful, and it directly affects our approach. The illusory truth affect is a great example of the power of the mind. It's amazing, but simple – the more your team hears something, the more they believe it to be true – even if they know it isn't. I made sure to share the data with my guys about the third matchup between two teams. I was intentionally fighting the natural mentality to believe what we hear.

In my nine years at RIC we were in that scenario 12 times, where we had beaten a team twice and we had to play them again in the post-season. We were 11-1 in those twelve games.

Go with Your Best

The Murray Center was on fire that Friday night as you'd expect. We had become a pretty good local story in an area where college basketball is really important. We had a lot of students on hand along with the rest of the RIC community. The building was alive and intense – the kind of atmosphere great competitors earned the right to play in.

We knew UMass-Dartmouth was good enough to beat us, but we also knew we were the better team. We came out early and played like it, getting out to a lead and controlling the game. For most of the first half, we were ahead 8-12 points. With about nine minutes to go in the first half, up by 11, Kinsey Durgin picked up his second foul.

Conventional wisdom has always said that when one of your key players gets his second foul in the first half, you put him on the bench. You don't want him to get a third foul in the first half—even though halftime seems like a pretty arbitrary mile marker. With twenty-two minutes left he can't play, but with twenty minutes left he's good to go the rest of the way? While this way of thinking has certainly been challenged more recently in college basketball, as a young head coach, I still believed what I heard the most—the illusory truth effect in full swing.

I put Kinsey on the bench, and we started to struggle. Dartmouth battled back to get within five points with a couple of minutes to play in the half. I was just hoping to get to halftime without losing any more ground, and I kept Kinsey on the bench. But we struggled without him. We went into halftime with a three-point lead, and Kinsey had only played nine minutes. We had lost control of a game we had a firm grip on. We let Dartmouth up off the mat.

Luckily for me, Kinsey and his teammates bailed me out in the second half. He came out and played great, the best player in the gym. We regained control, and although it was never a blowout, we finished it off without too much stress in the closing minutes. After the game, I looked at the box score and saw that Kinsey was clearly the best player on the floor with 21 points, but he had only played 23 minutes. I shook my head. When the game started to slip away in the first half, I left the best player on the bench with two fouls for nine minutes. It almost cost us.

I had the best player in the building, and I had only played him slightly more than half of the game in or a do-or-die scenario. We started to lose control of the game in the first half, with Kinsey on the bench. It was the mistake of a young coach. I thought more about conventional wisdom than what my team needed. We could have lost the game, with the best player only playing half of it.

From that point forward, I made sure we always went with our best. Had we lost that game, it would have been because I didn't give us the best chance to win. Yes, there is some risk to putting Kinsey back in and getting into foul trouble, but that can be managed. Losing control with him on the bench cannot.

It seems like a simple concept, but sometimes in practice it isn't so easy. Make sure you go with your best in an important spot. We often include soft factors with regards to our leadership approach – how are certain people going to feel, keeping people happy, following the conventional route – that shouldn't get in the way of decision making in a big moment. I'm not saying the feelings of your team aren't important, because clearly, I believe they are. And the task at hand may present unique challenges. But make sure when the task is complete, you've put your best foot forward.

I learned that lesson in our semi-final game against UMass-Dartmouth. Fortunately, it was a lesson learned in a win.

Quick Turnaround

There wasn't a lot of time between the semi-finals and the finals, so we really didn't have time to celebrate or prepare. The semi-finals were on Friday night and the finals were on Saturday at 2:00. We were now 23-3 and our guys were obviously pumped to be playing for a championship. To the surprise of no one, our opponent in the finals would be Keene State.

The fact that it was such a quick turnaround probably helped me. This was my first moment as a head coach in a really big game. I didn't have much time to think. I just stayed invested in my team. In a spot like that, the tendency is to over coach, to get too specific. It's a huge game, so you want to make sure every detail is covered. That can paralyze your team.

We didn't have time for that. I told my team repeatedly that I wanted playmakers on the floor in the post-season, and now I had to let them play. I didn't have much choice. There was no time to think, and that was a good thing. I stayed focused on our mentality because that was all we had time for. We knew Keene very well and they knew us, so there wasn't a lot of strategy to discuss. I wanted to make sure our heads were in the right place.

Before we left the building Friday night, I told the team to go home and think about cutting down the nets. I wanted them to sense what it would feel like to win a championship. Keene had beaten us twice, and I knew we weren't going to be cocky. We had a very business-like approach the entire second semester, and I trusted that would continue. I wanted us to be aggressive and confident, and I wanted that picture of cutting down the nets in their head.

Fight the urge to overthink it in a big situation. Trust your team and their preparation and turn them loose. That trust you have in them is a powerful force.

Connect to Your Core
February 24th, 2007 – Championship Saturday

When I showed up to the building the next day, I could literally feel the pressure. The reality of what was about to happen was right in front of us. Playing for a championship, a spot in the NCAA Tournament, and literally making history. I don't know if our guys felt the pressure as I did, but I wanted to make sure to loosen them up. Probably because I needed to loosen up.

Until that point the Little East Conference was almost always a one-bid league. The team that won the conference tournament went to the national tournament, and everyone else went home. There were over 400 division III teams in the country and getting an at-large bid was very hard.

I realized afterwards that we would have most likely gotten an at-large bid with a loss, but at the time we didn't really know. It felt like a must win. Before the game I wanted to break the tension. I needed a way to loosen everybody up, to free our guys up to play without fear. I needed to free myself up from thinking about the result.

I didn't want to talk to the team for too long. That would probably just add to the tension. I wanted to get us mentally right. I waited longer than I usually would and got into our meeting room a little late.

"We are going to the NCAA Tournament," was the first thing I said. "We are in. You guys have done it. We'll be the first RIC team to play for an NCAA Championship in 30 years. Regardless of what happens today, we are going. We are going to hang a banner in that gym, and you guys will, as a team, walk together forever. I just want you to know how proud I am to be your coach."

I sensed a little bit of relief and definitely some surprise, because I don't think our guys were expecting to hear about the NCAA Tournament before this game. I wanted them to feel good about what we had accomplished. I wasn't sure I was right, but I wanted to take the pressure off.

"But this game is bigger than that," I continued. "This game is about pride. This game is about a team coming into our building and trying to beat us for the third straight time. This game is about how tough we are, both mentally and physically. This game is about who we are. That is so much more important than the result."

And with that, I turned around and took an eraser to the scouting report that was up on the chalk board. My assistant, Matt O'Brien, who was getting ready to deliver the scout, had a look on his face that said, "what the hell are you doing?" I didn't want to talk about Keene. Our opponent was irrelevant. It was about us.

My goal, again, was to separate my team from the result. I didn't want them thinking about what would happen if we won or lost. Compete without compromise, not driven by success or failure. Personal and team pride, and how we went about our business, was more important. I wanted them to play for each other, to count on each other. Were we really going to let our biggest rival beat us three times in one year, and cut down the nets in our building? Surely you won't let that happen to your teammates.

It's such a big part of a championship culture, and I know it's been pervasive throughout this book. Get your team to believe in something bigger than the results, and the results will follow. But if they are the driving force behind how you operate, you'll feel like you are missing something. Defining yourself by wins and losses is a shallow existence, and one that will eventually stop motivating your team. The best way to get the desired results is to separate your process from them.

I wanted to relieve the pressure, and I felt like separating from the results would help do that. I also wanted them thinking about something more important—which was who we were as a team. I wanted them locked in on the way we competed for one another, not what the scoreboard was going to say. Believe in each other like we have all year, and we'll be happy with the outcome.

To be honest, I still thought at that point Keene was a better team than us. They had beaten us twice, and neither one of them were flukes. They had outplayed us both times. I knew we were good enough to beat them, don't get me wrong, and I was confident we could do so. But I was very concerned. They were really good, and to that point I wasn't sure we were quite at their level.

Well, our guys changed my mind on that as soon as the ball went up. We controlled the game from the outset and were in charge the entire way. We played hard, smart, disciplined and loose. The game was never out of hand, we were always in control. If you had only watched that championship game, you would have thought we were clearly the better team. We expected to win from the tip. As the game played out, I marveled at our maturity and growth. We were the better team.

I took a lot of pride in not only how well we played that day, but how much we had grown as a team. We played with great confidence and poise. We looked like a championship team, one that had been there for years. It didn't take anything spectacular. We had trans-formed into a championship team right before my eyes, day by day, competing at a high level for each other. And due to my inexperi-ence as a head coach at that point, I didn't even realize it was happening.

The best thing I did that day was eliminate any fear or doubt from within our locker room, despite what I was feeling inside. The players took it from there. It was a surreal feeling on that sideline.

The horn went off and before you knew it, we were cutting down the nets. Rhode Island College, 2007 Little East Champs.

Championship Success

What a feeling. It's hard to describe how good it feels when you go through a full season with a team, handle the ups and downs, and win a championship. I knew what that group had been through, especially the six seniors, and it felt so good to share success with them. Those guys knew they'd have their own banner hanging in the Murray Center every time they came back. I felt excitement, joy, relief, satisfaction, pride—so many different emotions. A lot of emotions to handle moving forward, because we had more games to play.

We cut down the nets, did our TV interviews, and took a bunch of pictures with the team and with family. It seemed like we stayed on the floor forever. We were certainly going to celebrate this championship and enjoy every minute of it. But as we started to settle down, I had to start thinking about our mentality moving forward. As Winston Churchill said, "Success is never final." The challenge only grew bigger.

After the Iona win in the pre-season, we hadn't handled our emotions very well. But we learned that the way we felt after success would affect our approach. All of the emotion we felt—the joy, satisfaction, excitement and relief—would be part of our team moving forward. Once again, we needed an intentional mentality about what we accomplished and how to handle it.

We won the tournament on a Saturday, and the NCAA doesn't reveal the DIII brackets until Monday at noon, so we had a full day to enjoy our success without even knowing who we'd be playing. That gave me a day to settle down and figure out an approach. I spoke to the guys briefly after the game and our celebration.

"Go home tonight and think about winning the national championship." I could see their eyes light up. "Think about winning the whole thing. Because I'm telling you right now, we are good enough. We are good enough to win it all. There are 60 teams left with a chance to win a national title, and Rhode Island College is one of them. You guys have earned that."

I didn't want them just thinking about what it would be like to play in the NCAA Tournament. I wanted them to think about winning it. We had no opponent to prepare for and we wouldn't until Monday afternoon. Our confidence was at an all-time high and I wanted that to continue.

I also wanted to set a deadline for when we mentally had to get back to work. I told them when we woke up on Monday, we were back to the basics. Get better today, win our next game. At that point we would no longer be thinking about winning it all or thinking about Keene State and the Little East Championship. It was going to be a regular Monday.

I wanted to draw a line. When you experience success, you have to celebrate it and enjoy it. It's a big part of the reward for all of the work. Feeling great about your accomplishments will help motivate you moving forward. But there is always more work to do. Drawing a mental line in the sand helped us compartmentalize the emotion. Practice on Monday would be at 4:00 just like it always was, and we had a lot of work to do.

NINE

ELITE SUCCESS

MARCH 2005 (NCAA TOURNAMENT)

A t the division III level, there are no selection Sunday parties. The bracket is released online by the NCAA at noon on Monday, and with our guys class and work schedules, getting everyone together to watch just didn't make sense. Our staff watched it in the office, and the players were in their rooms or somewhere on campus hitting refresh on their phones to see if the bracket was out yet. This approach kind of fit the low maintenance DIII model, and certainly fit the blue-collar ethos of our program. Just tell us when and where and let us get back to work.

We got a little more good news on Monday when we found out our matchup. We were also selected as a host school, so we'd be hosting a four-team pod the following Friday and Saturday, just like we had with the Little East Tournament. We would be matched up against Coast Guard, and the other game was between Trinity and Brandeis, in the Murray Center on Friday night.

Rest

Our guys were focused and ready to go on Monday, as I had expected. We put the championship game behind us, and we were excited about what was in front of us. I felt it was a great time to get after them. We had four days before we played again, we had Sunday off, and we were feeling good. It was a great time to drive them harder than I ever had. When you have success, push your team for more. Don't let them settle for what has already been accomplished. It's a great way to avoid the complacency that can unknowingly set in when you win. That Monday was a time for me to let them know I expected more out of them. Being good enough to win our league wasn't good enough anymore. Competing for a national championship was a different level.

I also wanted to get a lot of rest. I have never been a big fan of having walk-throughs or light shooting days at practice. We challenged our guys mentally every day, and often we needed a mental break more than a physical one. I know I did at times. If we were on the court, we were always going to compete at a high level. I never wanted my team to expect, or accept, anything less. We didn't have light days at practice. If we needed a day off to rest, we'd take the day off.

We got after it really good on Monday, but we took Tuesday off. I don't think our guys were expecting that, nor do I think too many coaches were taking a day off during NCAA Tournament week. But we hadn't had four straight days of practice since the beginning of January. And if we did what we expected, we'd have to play back to back games to get to the Sweet 16 on Friday and Saturday. I didn't want that Saturday game to be our sixth straight day on the court. I thought more rest would help us play better.

The common approach as a leader is to drive your team harder when the stakes get higher. But that can work against you. Getting more out of them does not have to mean spending more time at work. You may feel like you want your team to work more, but that may not be what they need. It's so important to take the pulse of your team every day and understand what is best for them. If you trust the way your team prepares, oftentimes less is more.

The tendency to overdo it, especially in a big spot, is real. Don't be afraid to take a different path if it fits the approach of your group. More teams suffer from overuse than they do from too much rest. And the mental rest is as important as the physical. Giving your team a break is an intentional approach to improvement, an approach that many of us fail to recognize.

Body Language – What Really Matters?
NCAA Tournament, Round 1

When Friday finally arrived, I knew we were ready. We had a great three days of practice and we were confident we were better than Coast Guard (remember, we had beaten them at their place in December). The only thing I was worried about was our nerves. It wasn't easy to predict how we'd respond to playing in the NCAA Tournament.

We had a great atmosphere in the gym, made better when six busloads of Coast Guard Academy cadets showed up to cheer on their classmates. Our guys enjoyed the environment and so did Coast Guard, with both teams playing well. It was a really competitive, well played NCAA Tournament game. We held the lead most of the way.

While I was doing everything to make sure our guys were mentally prepared, my inexperience as a head coach in this spot probably hurt us. As the second half moved on and we couldn't pull away to a comfortable lead, I got tight. Normally we played ten or 11 guys, but I got out of character and shortened our bench. Usually midway through the second half I'd rest a couple of starters to make sure they were fresh down the stretch.

But we couldn't take control, and I left my starters on the floor, hoping we could pull away. I didn't get my key guys the right amount of rest and in an intense, emotional environment that had an impact. With about seven minutes to play, Kinsey Durgin took a

135

wide open pull-up three and banged it off the backboard. I realized he was dead tired, and I had to get him out. Tirrell Hill missed an open 15-footer badly, and I realized he was tired as well. I had been thinking I'd ride the game out with them on the floor, but I had left them on the floor too long. I had changed my approach under pressure, a leadership mistake from a young coach.

I had to get them a breather. I took Kinsey out first and gave him a quick break, and then put him back in for Tirrell. When Tirrell came out, he really wasn't happy. He had just thrown up a brick, we were only up by three points, and he didn't want to come off the floor. Tirrell was a great competitor, and he always wanted to be on the court. His body language showed he was clearly unhappy.

I went right over to Tirrell and told him it was my fault, that I had left him on the floor too long without getting him a break. Then I told him he was going to go back in quickly, and he was going to help us win the game. He needed a quick blow. He listened, but he was still frustrated. He wanted to be on the court. I wanted to get his mind right.

The best thing I did was ignore his body language. I didn't react to it, partially because his fatigue was my fault, but also because we had more important things to worry about. We had a game to win. I stayed focused on what really mattered to my team at that point. Under pressure, it's easy to get agitated by stuff that's not important. For basketball coaches, body language is often one of those things. We look at negative body language and come to conclusions, and often times those conclusions are either incorrect or irrelevant.

Tirrell was frustrated because he hadn't been playing great, we couldn't take control of the game, and he didn't want to come out. I understood that. His body language wasn't a message to me, or him "showing me up" as a coach. It wasn't personal. He was tired and frustrated and I needed to help him deal with that.

I've learned to coach the behavior, not the personality. It's not like I'm a fan of negative body language, but I don't make a big deal out of it. I'm sure my body language wasn't great at that point in the game either. On top of that, body language can be hard to read. I'm just not very good at it. It's easy to come to the wrong conclusion. If bad body language leads to bad behavior, then I'm going to address it.

There are plenty of little things that might aggravate you but don't really have a big impact on your team. Remember, it's about what they need, not what you feel. Body language is simply one data point that may give you insight into what is happening with a player. And it's hardly the most important one. Their behavior is much more valuable to you than how they look doing it. Body language can be more about control – I want you to act a certain way, don't show me up! – than about the impact on your team. If it is a sign of bad behavior that is affecting your team, then address the behavior.

Had I been worried about Tirrell's body language I probably would have left him on the bench. But he was a huge part of our team and we needed him. His frustration didn't bother me; it was my job to get him right. I settled him down, and after a quick two minute rest, I put him back in. He made several key plays down the stretch, as he usually did, and we won the game.

After our first NCAA Tournament win in almost 30 years, we were now 25-3.

Mental Toughness

The NCAA Tournament offered a little more time to celebrate a victory than the conference tournament, but not much. If you won on Friday, you played on Saturday, but the game wasn't until the evening. We had a few extra hours to catch our breath, but still limited time to prepare. We were going to play Brandeis, who had knocked off Trinity, for the chance to go to the Sweet 16.

Toughness was a core value in our program, and Jack Clark, the great rugby coach at Cal, had a simple definition for mental toughness that we adopted – "the ability to move on to the next most important thing." That definition fit our core ethos very well. We talked about being mentally tough all of the time, so I figured we'd better define it and attach behaviors to it. We needed to move on to the next most important thing—Brandeis.

I learned in my years as an assistant coach that we used a lot of "buzzwords" in coaching, words that sounded right and felt important, but ones that we didn't define. We talked about values like leadership, toughness and competing constantly, but we didn't always show our players what it looked like. I didn't want to just tell my team to be mentally tough; I wanted them to see what it looked like.

We talked about being mentally tough enough to move on to the next most important thing. That was our challenge. We had done it after each win in the conference tournament. We locked in on what we needed to do to get better. We all felt great that we had just won an NCAA Tournament game in a gym packed with friends and family. But our behavior now—the way we prepared for Brandeis— would define how tough we really were.

Core Values

As I've discussed, I'm a believer in core values for organizations. I just think sometimes we get our approach to them wrong. I've talked at length about defining values as behaviors, and that became a significant part of our approach at RIC. You want your core values to come alive for your organization. Connecting those values to specific behavior has a powerful impact on developing and maintaining an elite culture.

The second mistake leaders often make with core values, and I certainly did when I first became a head coach, is we have too many of them. When we think about what's important to us, we end up with broad thoughts on our philosophy. And it's usually too much. Your philosophy and your core values are different. Your philosophy is your overall approach, and your team will see it and live it every day. Your core values are a shared set of beliefs that you should be able to define as behaviors. They should be short, distinct and worth fighting for.

A three-page list of bullet points about how you will handle things every day is more of an operating manual than a set of core values. Pick a few important values—three is usually the right number for me—that are broad and easy to define to fit your approach. Make sure they are important to you, reflect who you are, and simple to define. Get your team to understand them and believe in them. The behaviors that represent those core values will be important to them, worth fighting for. When we have too many core values, none of them really define us, and the impact will be limited.

Belief in Your Core Values

I knew we'd need to be mentally tough to beat Brandeis that next night. It's a great feeling winning an NCAA Tournament game, but also a bit of an odd one. Relief and satisfaction run through you after a week of preparation for the biggest game of the year, but then you wake up and realize you are forty minutes away from being one of 16 teams left competing for the national championship. It's exhilarating.

We came out loose and prepared against Brandeis, and we played very well. We were the better team from the start and built an 18-point lead with about seven minutes to play. We had that mature, composed look of a championship team playing at home. We were playing great, cruising towards the Sweet 16.

And then we weren't. Somehow, we just stopped scoring. I'm not sure what happened, we just gradually started missing shots and

Brandeis made a few plays. We couldn't put the ball in the hoop and our lead started to fade. The clock looked like it was moving the wrong way.

I was proud of the way we handled that game as we started to struggle. We were mentally tough, moving on to the next play. When we couldn't score down the stretch, we stayed connected to the core of what made us good. We were great defensively. In the huddles, our guys stayed positive with each other and talked about getting stops, not worrying about all of the missed shots. It was a display of mental toughness and a rock-solid belief in the core of who we were.

We only scored one point in the final seven minutes of the game, and it was on a free throw from Kamari Williams with under a minute to play. But it was enough to win the game. While the last seven minutes of that game may not have been pretty basketball, it was beautiful from a leadership and team culture standpoint.

We were 26-3 and headed to the Sweet Sixteen.

"Practice on Monday Is at 4:00"

Knowing that we were heading into our first win-or-go-home weekend to start the NCAA Tournament, I told our team on Thursday – our last practice before the first round – that practice on Monday was at 4:00. It was a simple, subtle reminder to them that I believed in them, and I expected to keep playing. I said it at half-time, and I repeated it in the huddles down the stretch. If we were struggling, I would ask them the question to get them to say it, "What time is practice on Monday?" And they would yell, "Four o'clock!"

Again, the most powerful thing you can do as a leader is make sure your team knows you believe in them. They want and need to hear that constantly, no matter how much you demand. You can hold them accountable in a way that reinforces your belief in them, without being negative. Remember that conversation I had with

Kinsey Durgin in January where he told me the guys felt I might be giving up on them? From that day I made sure that no matter how demanding I was, they always knew I believed in them.

When we got together after the Brandeis win, the message was simple: Practice on Monday is at four o'clock. The room went crazy. There were 16 teams left in the country with a chance to win the national championship, and Rhode Island College was one of them.

Oddly enough, at that time the NCAA division III Tournament was almost all completely regional to limit expenses and travel. They did not put out a full bracket like the division I tournament does – they only put out the first weekend matchups. They waited to see who won the games so they could matchup the teams that fit the best geographically (yes, really, they did this in the national championship). They have changed this since that point and now they have a bracket set from the beginning of the tournament. But in 2007, when you won two games in the tournament, you didn't know who you were going to play until the NCAA committee decided the matchups the next day.

We knew we were still playing; we just didn't know who or where. I told our guys again to go home, enjoy it, and think about winning the national championship. Our opponent, it turns out, would be very familiar.

Competitive Excellence

We found out on Sunday that we'd be heading to Amherst to play, and our opponent would be Keene State. Keene had gotten an at-large bid and gone to Salem State and beaten the host on a shot at the buzzer to advance to the Sweet 16.

It would be our fourth game against Keene that season, and our seventh time playing them over two years. After splitting with them in the regular season our first year, we had gone to Keene in the semi-finals of the ECAC post-season tournament and beaten them –

a game we won by 40. This year, they had beaten us twice but then we took them out in the LEC title game. We had split the first six games. I told our guys this would be game seven. As you can imagine, it wasn't too hard to get them excited.

I wanted to do two things mentally for our guys, which is why I referred to this one as game seven. I wanted to take the focus off the big picture, that we were just two games away from going to the Final Four, and just lock into a task that we were very familiar with —preparing to beat Keene State. I also wanted to avoid the conversation that we now had to beat Keene State for the second time in two weeks, a job that mentally might seem like a bigger challenge than just winning one game.

I wanted to sharpen our focus and alleviate the pressure. Game seven allowed for the fact that it was obviously a huge game, but also hopefully kept our attention on the task—this was us trying to beat Keene in one game. It was nothing more than that, and we had nothing else to look forward to. I was reading my team and trying to tap into their confidence. I wanted the pressure of the moment to add to that confidence, not take from it.

My team knew how big this moment was and I didn't need to make it any bigger. I knew they felt a ton of pressure because I could feel it. Privately, I wasn't thrilled about playing Keene again. Win or lose, we were in the middle of the greatest year our school ever had in basketball. But imagine if that year ends with a loss to your biggest conference rival – for the third time. It's hard to celebrate a great year when your conference rival ends your season and moves on. I felt that pressure, and I know our guys did too. A loss to anyone else and we would have celebrated the season forever. A loss to Keene and there would always be a bad taste in our mouths associated with the way it ended. Again, I needed to keep the pressure I felt away from my team.

Game seven was my approach to doing that. We prepared that week with a great balance of confidence and competitive excellence.

Competing was a core value for us, but as the season went on and we matured, I realized there was more to it than just playing hard. For us, competing was giving your best effort all of the time. But competing at a high level brought with it a lot of emotion, and that emotion had to be dealt with. It's really hard to lay it all on the line because you have to deal with the consequences – and you might lose. Competitive excellence is not only giving your best effort all of the time but handling the emotions that go along with that. It's a combination of intensity, edge, poise and composure. Our team had gone from learning how to compete—in January of year one, after the West Conn game—to competitive excellence.

Staying with Your Process

Amherst was hosting the regional, so neither us nor Keene had a home court advantage. Their campus was close enough to both of us that the gym was packed with fans from both sides. The place was on fire.

As you'd expect, when the ball went up, the compete level was very high. It was a close game, back and forth through most of the first half. Keene got ahead of us in the second half before we started making some plays down the stretch to take the lead. It looked, once again, like we knew we were supposed to win. We were tough and showed great composure, as did Keene. The game would come down to the final minute.

We had a two-point lead with twelve seconds left, and Keene had the ball. They needed a bucket; we needed a stop. I can still see, clear as day, David Sontag, Keene's first team all-league shooting guard, dribbling up the right side of the floor past our bench with the clock running down. He pulled up for a quick-trigger three that would give them the lead, and it looked pure the entire way. Fortunately, for us, it hit the front rim and came off the glass, and we were able to grab the rebound. We'd go the other way with less than three seconds left to shoot free throws and put the game away.

It was a perfect example of why the process is so much more valuable to your culture than the result. We were up two with the clock running out and Keene had the ball in the hands of their best player with a chance to win the game. Our defense was set, but he did get a look he could make. I thought it was going in the entire time the ball was in the air. But it glanced off the rim and we got the rebound. If that shot goes in, Keene heads on to the Elite Eight. It didn't, so we moved on. When that ball was in the air, neither team had any control over the result. So how can you let that result define you?

We had won game seven against Keene State in the final seconds. We were now 27-3 and headed to the Elite Eight.

The excitement in our locker room was through the roof. It was one of those "just lucky to be a part of it" games, and we were very fortunate to come out on top. What we were doing was special, and we knew it. I wanted to celebrate. I wanted our players to enjoy it. My approach was the same, to ride their confidence and stay out of the way. We were going to play for the right to go to the Final Four and I wanted them to enjoy every minute of it.

Again, without much time to prepare, I was really just worried about our guys mentally. And, truthfully, I didn't have too much to worry about there either. Our guys were feeling great, we were mentally tough, and we had already prepared for Amherst once about a month earlier. We knew they were a great team, but we had come to terms with the fact that we were a great team as well. There were only eight teams left standing.

We didn't have to do anything different. I didn't need to get our guys focused or bring them down from their high. We were locked in and feeling great. We were ready to play.

The Elite Eight
March 10, 2007 – At Amherst

The next night, I stood just outside the gym as our guys were warming up, listening to the crowd and the music. It felt like the building was going to explode. It gave me a minute to think about what we had accomplished, and how proud I was to be a part of that team. The environment was incredible, and I made sure to remind our guys that they had earned the right to be there. Mentally, we were ready to go; there wasn't a doubt in my mind.

The only issue was that Amherst was a great team, and they were ready to go as well. They came out and threw the first punch in the first half, playing with a level of toughness and intensity we hadn't really seen out of them before. We were a bit shell shocked. We fully expected to go toe to toe with them, but they were all over us. Their talent and size knocked us back a little bit, and they controlled the edge of the game.

As leaders, we are almost exclusively focused on our own group, and rightfully so. But it's easy to lose sight of external factors that can impact your team. We hadn't been ourselves, and I was upset about that. But there was a big reason why—it wasn't that we weren't ready to play or focused. It was because Amherst was *really* good. They were affecting our approach and deserved credit for that. We had to figure out how to handle it.

At halftime we were down by 11 and I wasn't happy because we hadn't been ourselves. We let Amherst dictate how the game was being played, and it had affected our compete level. We were playing hard, we always did, but we didn't have our usual competitive edge. Amherst was controlling that edge. We had defined ourselves with that edge and now we were losing that battle. I needed to snap our guys out of it.

The Way You Deliver the Message

The way you deliver the message—especially when things aren't going well for your organization—is often more important than the message itself. I'm not really a screamer by nature, and I tend to keep my composure as a coach because I want my team to do the same. Usually when I got after my guys it was a calculated decision, because I felt we needed a spark.

I thought a lot about my tone when I was delivering the message. If I'm always using the same tone, especially a loud one, the message turns into noise. The team will turn it off. There are times when you have to deliver a stern, sharp message and it might be a little louder than normal. That's okay. But if you aren't careful about how often you play that card, you can quickly lose your team. Remember, leadership isn't so much about what you say as it is about what they hear. The message they receive is on you. Be intentional about your tone to make sure your team can hear you.

I knew I had to get to my guys at halftime, so I walked in the locker room right behind them with a forceful tone. "They're good, fellas! What do you want me to do??? They're really good. They might beat us. But I'll be damned if they are going to beat us because we are afraid to compete. That's not who we are. If they are better than us, we'll live with that. But there is no way we are going to back down!" My tone was pretty intense, and the delivery was purposely loud. I walked out of the room.

I knew we needed a wake-up call, but I also knew we had to figure it out together. There may be times where your team needs to hear a difficult message and the tone has to be different, but they still need to know you are all in with them. I wanted to rattle my team, not because I was upset but because I felt that was what they needed. I left the room for a few minutes, but then I walked back in and calmly discussed the adjustments we needed to make to win the game. Don't be afraid to get after your team when they need it. But make sure they know you are still with them and give them what they need to succeed.

Our guys understood the message. Even a group that hung its hat on how hard we competed every day, the will to compete can sometimes be taken right out of you. We were a little shocked by how good they were in that first half, and it affected our approach. We were showing some fear in the way we competed, and that wasn't us. That needed to change.

And it did. We came out on fire in the second half and played with an intense competitive edge. We had a great approach. We jumped on them and battled back into the game, going toe to toe the entire second half. We cut the lead to four with under five minutes to play, but Amherst never wavered. They continued to play well and stood up to us, taking our best shot. We got big stops, we made big shots and we left everything we had on the floor. We had the ball late in the second half on four straight possessions with a chance to cut the lead to two, and we couldn't convert on any of them. We just couldn't get over the hump.

Full Measure

One memory is seared into my brain from that game. In the final minute, after we had missed on offense and had to foul to stop the clock, Amherst had a comfortable lead as they headed back to the foul line. The result was all but decided. Our guys walked back down the floor and Kinsey Durgin put his arm around Brian Stanko and slowly walked back to the foul line with him. Two of the six seniors who had been through so much over four years. They knew the ride was over. No regrets, no real sadness, just quietly appreciating each other in their last moment on the floor as teammates.

Those guys knew, as did everyone on our team, that they had left everything they had on the floor for each other. There was nothing left in the tank. We just weren't good enough. We called it full measure. Full measure was the ultimate gift of an elite team. It was the chance to prepare at a high level with your closest mates, and then lay everything you have on the line for them, knowing they are doing the same for you. At the end of the day, win or lose, you walk off the floor together, exhausted, knowing you've given everything you had for your teammates. That was full measure for RIC basketball.

Our season ended that night in a small gym in Western Massachusetts at 27-4. Amherst would go on to win the national championship. We headed back to Providence, having lost four games—two of them to the eventual national champions, and two of them to Keene State—another team that made the Sweet Sixteen. Yet we had beaten them twice as well, in the conference tournament and in that Sweet Sixteen. Not to mention we had beaten a division I team in an exhibition game.

The investment we made in each other that season turned into the ride of our lives. The journey was extremely rewarding and an incredible learning experience for me as a leader. At no point during that year did we ever feel like a dominant team, and maybe that was the beauty of it. We just went about our business the right way and continued to pile up the wins, but we never thought we were untouchable. Perhaps not knowing how good we were was a benefit for a group that had never seen that level of success. We never really felt like a dominant team until after Amherst had ended our season. We looked back and it was clear we had done something uncommon.

Our locker room that night after the Amherst game was a special place to be. There were tears for sure, but they were tears borne of pride and accomplishment. I never felt any sadness in the room about the loss. The sadness was about the journey coming to an end —we'd never get to compete together as a team again. But there was an electric connection in that locker room that made it a happy place to be, a strong sense that we had created something special. And we had bought into an uncommon approach to get there.

Despite the loss, it's one of the best post-game locker rooms I've ever been in. Those players, that team, those first two seasons all shaped my approach as a leader and taught me innumerable lessons about developing an elite culture. I'm not sure I realized how much I was learning along the way, because I was immersed in the approach. But I knew I was a part of something special. We had developed an elite, championship culture in just two years.

The challenge became how to sustain it.

TEN

SUSTAINING ELITE SUCCESS

APRIL 2007

T he face of our program changed in 2007. From that point on, we all believed in how we went about our business. Success makes the buy-in a lot easier. The Elite Eight run eliminated any doubt. We were at a championship level and moving forward that would be the expectation.

An expectation of success is a key component of high achieving organizations. I told you how much I liked high expectations, and now they were set. It's not so much learning how to win. It's learning how to prepare. It's understanding the value of how you operate every day, and how that translates to success. Not just for your team, but in the big picture as well. The approach you take is not finite and doesn't end when you've achieved your organizational goals. It translates to success in the everyday lives of you and your teammates. When they start to see that, the buy-in becomes easier.

The challenge is that you can't expect success without experiencing it. This is why including your team in the process from the beginning is essential. Can you get them to believe in what you do before they experience the reward? The day-to-day has to be something they are aligned with. It doesn't mean it can't be challenging or you have to do it their way. It means their mentality and your organization's mentality have to connect. To create buy-in before you've experienced real success is one of the great challenges of leadership.

Establishing the program at a championship level felt great. We had accomplished something together that had never been done, and that's powerful. The legacy of that team will live forever at Rhode Island College. And it still has an impact on my approach every day.

We enjoyed the ride and took some time in the spring to relax and recharge. But eventually we had to move forward, and that meant handling everything that went along with success. The natural question that follows elite success is how do you sustain it?

Having been through it, I've learned that sustaining elite success is the ultimate challenge for any organization. While I remain incredibly proud of that 2007 team and their legacy, I also take great pride in what we did moving forward. Eight straight NCAA Tournaments. Six LEC Tournament titles and five regular season titles. Three Sweet Sixteen appearances with that trip to the Elite Eight. We established a championship level culture and sustained it over nine years, at a place that had never experienced such success.

We went 125-27 in the Little East Conference, a winning percentage over 82%. Our record in the Little East Tournament was 21-3. We played in eight straight Little East Championship games after never having appeared in one prior to 2007. We won 204 games in nine years, with a winning percentage of almost 75%.

How did we do it? I can't say I knew at the time. I was fortunate to attract elite talent and great kids and we got them bought into the right culture. The success we had in 2007 certainly made that easier. But it wasn't so much about sustaining the winning as it was staying with our approach. When kids came to visit our program, they wanted to be a part of it. The way we competed, the positive environment, the open relationships the players had with one another and the coaches – it all added up. We developed an environment that attracted talented people who wanted to compete.

As we moved the program forward after 2007 there were some key components that played an important role in sustaining our level of success.

Define Yourself Clearly and Simply

You need a clear vision of who you want to be as an organization. And you have to make this clear and simple for your team.

Our first core value was "compete." That was how we defined ourselves. Our definition of competing was "your best effort always, without compromise." Nothing could get in the way of how hard we played. Ever.

The behavior was defined clearly every day. We celebrated competing in practice. The first one to dive on the floor for a loose ball. Sprinting back after a turnover. Keeping an offensive rebound alive. We showed the behaviors on film. There was no doubt about what competing looked like.

Define the core values and standards for your program clearly and in simple terms. Your values are who you are as a team—and you should define them as behaviors. Your standards are the benchmarks of your conduct. They are how you measure and evaluate what you do.

A clear vision of who you are, for everyone in your organization, is essential to sustain elite success.

Alignment

The culture of your organization needs to align with who you are, but also with the beliefs of your institution. If you are the President or CEO and you report to the board, your beliefs need to align with theirs. If you are a head coach, you need alignment with your athletic director and the school President. You also need to fill your team with people who are aligned. This doesn't mean you can't have differences of opinion. But your decisions should always be made with the vision and values of your organization in mind.

You have to be true to yourself. You also have to recruit and retain talent for your organization, and their comfort level is important. To do that in an environment where powerful influences are fighting over the direction of the program is very challenging—and I'd say unsustainable.

Live your culture every day. Your team will as well. They should be walking billboards for what you believe in. If you don't have alignment, and your culture isn't something worth fighting for to them, it will be difficult to achieve at a high level.

You can have some success with some outliers, but it will be hard to sustain it at an elite level without true alignment. Get everyone on board with your vision and values.

Culture First – Always

Do you remember the story of Benjy Nichols in my first off-season? He didn't want to run because his teammates had been missing class. He spoke up, and he walked away. He never played for us again.

That day was one of the most important days in establishing our culture. I was scared as it was happening, not knowing if it was going to cause a mutiny. And I hadn't planned it. But I stood firm on our culture, and what we were really about. We were going to handle ourselves a certain way off the court.

From that point forward, our guys knew that if they tested me (or what we believed in) that I wouldn't flinch. You have to be willing to sacrifice talent for your culture. In fact, if you don't at some point lose someone talented who isn't really bought in to your culture, something is probably wrong. The sacrifice necessary for elite success is not for everyone.

Always put your culture first. That means making some very tough decisions and losing some talent that you feel can help your team. In the short term, it can be very hard. But over the long haul, any cracks in your culture will be devastating and almost impossible to overcome.

Create Ownership

The idea of ownership is all over this book because my teams at Rhode Island College showed me how it translates to sustained, elite success. Ownership is in the fabric of high performing teams. A lack of ownership is one of the most common differences between good teams and elite teams.

Your values, your standards, and your overall culture—they need to be things that are worth fighting for. To be willing to fight for it, it has to be theirs. It can't just be something they hear from the boss every day. They have to own it.

Creating ownership comes down to how much control you are willing to give up. You are the leader, and you set the tone and guide the process. But let your players own it. Ask a lot of questions and listen as much as you can. Ask them about the core values and how they would define them. When something doesn't meet your standards, don't declare that what they did isn't good enough. Ask questions: Is that good enough for us? Does that meet our standard? What are we going to do about it?

Don't just get them to buy into what you believe. Get them to tell you what they believe. Get them to talk and be willing to listen. It's extremely powerful when you can say to your group, "this is what you told me you wanted," when something hard is on the horizon. It's just as powerful when they hold each other accountable to your standards before you do. They will learn to compete for one another, and the strength of that approach will carry your culture.

The Value of Talent

With all the talk of the importance of culture, it's easy to forget about the talent. Getting buy-in to the difficult stuff you need to do to win big is significantly easier if they are capable of meeting your demands. Talented individuals can do the hard stuff easier, and when they realize they can do it, they'll buy into it quicker.

It seems obvious that to sustain a high level of success, you need to have talent. But it gets overlooked more than you think. Not every person you hire, or recruit, is going to be a foot soldier for your values or a great culture guy. But they might be able to consistently perform, and that's also really important.

Look for natural talent. Guys who make difficult tasks look comfortable, and guys who can adjust on the fly with ease. The right fit for your culture can't be the only measure. Acquire the talent to succeed, and it will help advance your culture more than you think.

If your culture is right and your players take ownership of it, you can absorb some talent that isn't as naturally bought in to your approach. The strength of your culture and the leadership of your team will give you a feel for who you can take and how they'll fit. You need talent to sustain success and advance your culture. Don't take that for granted.

Not Good Enough

The flip side to the talent paradigm is to make sure you have some teammates who "aren't good enough." I'll explain to you what I mean.

At RIC I was blessed with a number of talented players who we didn't recruit, Cam Stewart, for example, a key member of our Elite Eight run. Some of them showed up unknowingly. We always had a tryout to give kids a chance, and I started to notice a trend. Not only did we usually keep a couple of those guys every year, one or two of them would usually find their way into the lineup. They became key players for us.

Cameron Stewart. Nick Manson. Darius Debnam. Ethan Gaye. Jacob Page. These weren't just good teammates who competed hard in practice. They started for us in NCAA Tournaments. Manson and

Debnam started on back-to-back Sweet 16 teams, and I didn't recruit either one of them. Darius actually came to RIC *after we told him we didn't think he was good enough, and we wouldn't have room for him.* He was a two-year captain on Sweet 16 teams. Think about that for a second. Cam Stewart scored almost 1,000 points in his career.

The guys who "weren't good enough," so to speak, did so much to drive our culture. They were the glue to it. We had some elite talent and that was a big part of our success. But the program kids, the ones who had to fight and scratch for their place on the team every day – they were the ones most responsible for our approach. And it was the approach that made our success sustainable. Their hunger, commitment and toughness drove our organization.

John Beilein always said, "Never underestimate the value of a low-maintenance player." We made it a point to find room for kids who were dying to be a part of it. It mattered to us a lot, and it should matter to you. Find a place within your organization for people with something to prove and reward their contributions. They will become the heartbeat of your team.

Be Flexible

Our championship culture was always fluid. It was constantly evolving, as was my approach. We had our basic core values, but that didn't mean we were averse to trying something new. If you aren't adapting, you aren't getting better. You are likely getting worse.

In my seventh year at RIC, the dynamics of our roster had changed. We lost the best point guard in the league, Antone Gray, who was also the best leader I had ever coached. He led us to back-to-back Sweet Sixteens and four straight NCAA Tournaments. While we still had talent, our two best players that next year were forwards, and my new point guard was more of a tough, physical player than a jet.

We were a fast team that liked to play in transition and go off the dribble, but our personnel didn't fit that style anymore. Our three best players all were physical and got their work done inside. So instead of our wide open, dribble-drive attack, we went to a flex offense—a structured approach that relied on simple screens and pattern passing. I was never a big fan of the flex because I didn't like the spacing, and I wanted our guards to have room to create. But it fit our personnel better that year, so in year seven, as a head coach, we made a major change. We went on to advance to the second round of the NCAA Tournament, running an offense I really didn't like. But I was flexible enough to make a major change to fit our personnel.

The most dangerous phrase for organizational success is "because that's how we've always done it." If you aren't adapting, you are getting worse. You can stick to your core values and still be flexible. It's one of the toughest challenges you'll face, but it's essential to sustain success.

Be Consistent

Be flexible and consistent? Sounds like a contradiction, but it isn't.

The reason why your culture has to be clearly defined and explained, and aligned with everything you believe in, is because your players need to see you living it. They have to see it in your behavior. When they see that, they'll know how much it really means to you, and it will mean more to them.

You must be consistent. Your team is smart, and you aren't going to fool them. They don't have to hear it to know it. Your culture has to be who you are, and you have to live it on and off the court, in season and out. You can do it and still make the necessary changes to be successful.

A consistent approach with a flexible mindset can certainly work. Inconsistency in your approach will create cracks in your culture that you'll never be able to repair. Be consistent in how you live your culture every day.

Fight Entitlement Aggressively

After our Elite Eight run in 2007, I wanted our players to own our success. High expectations were part of the deal and we needed to handle the pressure of being the best. Our warmup shirts had "The Champ Is Here" on the back of them, and we took the floor at the Murray Center to the Jadakiss song of the same name. We talked about being the best team in the league. We prepared that way and carried ourselves that way—with confidence and class. We were picked to finish first in our league in eight of our nine years, and we embraced it every year.

Along with that confidence and the success came a sense of entitlement. We expected success to happen to us, and we lost some awareness of the approach necessary to achieve it.

Entitlement is poison for elite cultures. It can get into your system without much notice and it gradually erodes the foundation of your success. As a leader, you must have your radar up and expect it. The confidence that comes with achievement naturally evolves into an expectation of success, and the process can easily suffer. Adapting and staying ahead of the curve is critical.

We started to take for granted what we had built, and I had to fight the entitled mentality aggressively. We no longer appreciated what we had done, or what it would take to maintain it. We talked about what was important to us. Were we happy with one championship or did we want to sustain an elite level of success? Did we want to do it again?

I reminded our guys every day how lucky we were to be a part of something special. We had long conversations about it. We celebrated our competitive excellence and recognized our commitment to one another. We appreciated the people around us who helped us achieve our goals. Winning a championship wasn't a defining moment for us. The preparation would define us. Not just as a team, but for the rest of our lives.

When I asked my team how they felt about our program, the one word that kept coming up was "grateful." Grateful to be a part of it. Grateful to have my teammates. Grateful for the opportunity.

Being grateful was a perfect way to combat entitlement creeping into our program. As we moved forward, we decided we would be "Grateful for everything, entitled to nothing." It became the core of our program.

Recognizing and aggressively combating the entitlement that came along with our success allowed us to sustain it for nine years.

ELEVEN

IT HAS TO BE THEIRS

CONCLUSION

I said it to my team early in 2007 and I found myself repeating it constantly.

"Understand what we are doing here is special. This isn't happening everywhere. It's uncommon. Let's embrace it and enjoy it.

I recognized it then, and I still believe it to this day. I don't think I'll ever be a part of a culture as strong as the one we developed at Rhode Island College.

I had a vision of how I wanted it to look when I took over, but that vision was surpassed by a wide margin due to the players in our program. We created an environment that gave us a chance to be successful, but then I stepped to the side and let the players develop it and maintain it. That was the uncommon approach. It was theirs, and that made it really powerful. The best thing I did was help establish standards and then turn it over to my players. My leadership style was not about having control, but about giving it up and empowering those around me.

Culture and leadership are highly contextual. The situation you are in matters and may dictate a different approach. I found the right process for myself, and it fit perfectly with the school, the community and the kids in the gym. It was a great fit for me. To think there is one approach to leadership that fits everywhere is way too simple.

What worked specific to Rhode Island College in 2005 might not fit your organization today. Some ideas might need to be tweaked to fit your goals and your personnel, not to mention your personality. But the core of who you are as an organization and what you believe in as a leader have to be connected. And when they are, be relentlessly consistent in your belief and your execution. When you find the right combination, and add the right talent, special things can happen.

Our culture was based on trust and competitive excellence, but I didn't build it as much as it was built around me. Our players taught me as much about a championship culture as I taught them, and that was not what I expected. They believed in the core values we put in place, and they turned them into living, breathing behaviors that they fought for each day – and still do today.

Empower your people to be decision makers. The less control you have as a leader, the more power you give to your team, the better your chances for success. That's the real key to leadership in an elite culture. It may be set in place and directed by the leader, but it is built, maintained and nurtured by the participants.

Success for Rhode Island College basketball will always be connected to the players on that 2007 team, who were willing to buy into an uncommon approach and a demanding process. It wasn't always easy, and the progress was far from linear. We challenged them to compete at an elite level every day, to give more than they thought they could. They challenged me the same way, with their belief, effort, and commitment. In the process, they gave me the respect they felt I had earned and the room I needed to grow. They taught me how to be an effective leader.

I'm honored to walk with them forever.

TWELVE

STATISTICS

RHODE ISLAND COLLEGE BASKETBALL
2005-2014

WINNING IS A HABIT!

Rhode Island College
204 Wins in 9 years: most winning period in school history (204-63, .764)
125-27 Overall Record vs. Little East Competition (.822)
102-24 Little East Conference regular season record (.810) • 13-1 LEC record in 2008-09, 2012-13 – best in school history
48-16 Little East Road Record (.750)
58-8 Little East Home Record (.879)
34-12 (.739) post-season record • 22-3 LEC Tournament record • 10-8 NCAA Tournament record • 2-1 ECAC Tournament record
Appeared in 8 straight LEC Tournament Championship games – LEC Record • First tournament game appearances in school history
First Outright Little East Championships in school history • 2007, 2009, 2010, 2011, 2013 Regular Season Champions • 2007, 2008, 2010, 2011, 2013, 2014 Tournament Champions
Two Division I Wins • RIC 71, Iona 62 – November 4th, 2006 • RIC 61, Holy Cross 60 – November 1st, 2007
Sam Schonfeld Team Sportsmanship Award (2007) • Awarded by basketball officials
3 NCAA Sweet 16s – 1 Elite 8
Best season start in school history – 15-1 - 2006-07
Longest winning streak in school history – 14 - 2008-09
Highest final national ranking in school history - #11 – 2006-07
Hosted NCAA Tournament - first time in school history – 2007, 2009, 2013, 2014 • Games shown live on local cable television

RHODE ISLAND COLLEGE

MEN'S BASKETBALL DYNASTY
2005-2014

YEAR	RECORD	ACHIEVEMENTS
2013-14	20-9	LEC Tournament Champions NCAA 1st Round
2012-13	26-4	LEC Regular Season Tournament Champions NCAA 2nd Round
2011-12	23-7	NCAA Tournament 2nd Round
2010-11	21-8	LEC Regular Season Tournament Champions NCAA Sweet 16
2009-10	22-8	LEC Regular Season Tournament Champions NCAA Sweet 16
2008-09	23-6	LEC Regular Season Champions NCAA 1st Round
2007-08	23-7	LEC Tournament Champions NCAA 2nd Round
2006-07	27-4	LEC Regular Season Tournament Champions NCAA Elite Eight
2005-06	19-10	ECAC Finalist

9 YEARS   204-63 (.764)

RHODE ISLAND COLLEGE BASKETBALL 2005-14

BUILDING A CHAMPIONSHIP CULTURE

NUMBERS	2005-2014	1996-2005
Overall Record	204-63 (.764)	91-138 (.397)
Little East Conference	125-27 (.822)	44-80 (.355)
Post-Season Record	34-12 (.739)	4-7 (.364)
LEC Tournament Titles	6	0
LEC Regular Season Titles	5	1
NCAA Tournaments	8	0
NCAA Tournament Wins	10	0

THIRTEEN

MEMORIES IN PICTURES

A packed Murray Center crowd watches Rhode Island College take
on Keene State in the 2007 Little East Championship game.

Our six selfless seniors - Kamari Williams, Brian Stanko, Kinsey
Durgin, Tony Pierlioni, John Weir and Amde Tegbaru - Little East
Champions for the first time in school history.

Senior captain Kinsey Durgin after the Little East Championship win.

Kamari Williams enjoying a post-game interview as a champion, with some new neck-ware. May he rest in peace.

RIC wins the Sweet 16 "Game Seven" vs. Keene State and we are on to the Elite Eight.

Locked in, ready to take the floor against Amherst in the Elite Eight.

Our six seniors flashing their hardware.

Championship teams walk together forever.

Photographs courtesy of Lisa Weir at Autumn Studios - Instagram:
@autumnstudiosphotography

ACKNOWLEDGMENTS

To properly thank everyone who has helped me along the way would double the size of this book. While I will thank a few people specifically, understand that everyone I've come across, inside of a gym or out, has driven me to improve. For that I am sincerely thankful.

To my mother Evelyn, my father Don, and my brother John. Every decision I've made in my life, I've made with the both the courage and freedom to choose my own path, covered by your encouragement, love and support. Making you proud is still the fuel that drives me. I can never thank you enough.

To my wife Alicia, your friendship, caring heart, and unconditional love bring joy and purpose to my life every day. Your support for this book kept me moving forward. I love you.

To Tony Dottino, you've been a champion in my corner from the day we met. You have both supported and challenged my leadership approach in the best way possible. My sincerest thanks.

To Amy, Sarah, and Kristen, your intelligence, drive, and boundless spirit inspire me every day. Listen to your heart and follow your passion, always.

ACKNOWLEDGMENTS

A sincere thank you to Don Tencher, my athletic director at RIC, for trusting a first-time head coach with a different approach. None of this happens without your commitment and vision.

To Dr. John Nazarian and Dr. Nancy Carriuolo, your vision of the role athletics plays in the educational model will have an impact on the RIC student athletes for the rest of their lives. Thank you for your courage and support.

To the support staff at RIC—Jo-Ann D'Alessandro, Jeanne Dagostino, Gail Davis, Dolores Passarelli, Scott Gibbons, Scott Roy, Carlo Cantarella, Gerry Shellard, Tony Rainone, Andy Coughlin— your dedication to the student athletes is the glue that keeps the department together. Thank you for your investment every day.

To every coach I've ever worked with on a staff, I appreciate the way you challenged me to be better.

To all the players I've been lucky enough to share the court with— there are too many of you to name—thank you for your respect, your drive, and your passion. I love the way you've challenged me, and I hope you've learned from me the way I've learned from you.

The most important thank you goes to the players who laced them up every day for me at Rhode Island College. For believing in me, for investing as much as you did, for your passion, commitment, and trust. We created something truly special. I can't imagine being a part of a culture like that ever again. You took me on the ride of a lifetime and gave me an identity as a head coach. I'll go to battle with you any day of the week.

First whistle, on the floor.

ABOUT THE AUTHOR

Bob Walsh

Recognized as an innovative leader and team builder in the coaching world, Bob Walsh has been a college basketball coach for 28 years, including 13 years as a head coach. He's won over 60% of his games at both Rhode Island College and the University of Maine, including 11 league titles and eight trips to the NCAA Tournament.

The Founder and President of the Dynamic Leadership Group, Walsh has run the Dynamic Leadership Academy in Providence, RI since 2013 and is the host of the nationally recognized "Dynamic Leadership Podcast" on AthleticDirectorU.com. A popular speaker and clinician, Walsh delivers leadership training programs for coaches, teams, and corporations with an emphasis on high performance culture. His willingness to challenge traditional thought and his uncommon approach to leadership resonates with organizations interested in sustained elite performance.

A native of Larchmont, NY, Walsh attended Regis High School in Manhattan. He began his coaching career as a junior at Hamilton College in Clinton, NY, where he graduated in 1994. He received his master's degree in Mass Communications from Iona College in New Rochelle, NY in 1996. Walsh has made stops as an assistant at Iona, The University of San Diego, and Providence College. He was the head coach at Rhode Island College from 2005-14, and the University of Maine from 2014-18.

Walsh and his wife, Alicia, live in Newport, Rhode Island. He is currently on the basketball staff at Providence College.

Bob Walsh's Career and Statistics

Walsh was in charge of the Rhode Island College program from 2005-2014. He led a program that had not been to the NCAA Tournament in almost 30 years to eight straight trips, turning the Anchormen into a national power.

In nine seasons, Walsh led the Anchormen to a record of 204-63, including bids to the NCAA Tournament in the last eight. Rhode Island College was one of only five teams in the country to play in the NCAA Tournament every year from 2007-2014. Walsh led his squad to six Little East Conference Tournament Championships and five Regular Season Championships, with the 2007, 2010 and 2011, and 2013 squads earning both. The 2010 and 2011 Anchormen advanced to the NCAA Sweet 16, and the 2007 team advanced to the Elite 8, losing to eventual national champion Amherst. That team finished the season at 27-4, with the 27 wins setting a new

Rhode Island College record. The Anchormen were the only team in the New England Region of division III to be selected to eight straight NCAA Tournaments from 2007-14. Walsh was recognized as Coach of the Year eight times – three times as the Little East Coach of the Year (2007, 2009, 2013) and five times as the Rhode Island Sportswriters Coach of the Year (2007, 2009, 2010, 2013, 2014). In 2007, the Anchormen also received the Sam Schonfeld Sportsmanship award as voted on by the ECAC men's basketball officials.

The Anchormen set the standard in the Little East Conference, widely regarded as one of the toughest conferences in the country. The Anchormen posted a remarkable 125-27 record against Little East competition, a winning percentage of .822. They appeared in a conference record eight straight Little East Tournament Championship games, winning six of them, posting an overall record of 21-3 in LEC Tournament play. Prior to his arrival, the Anchormen had never appeared in a Little East Tournament Championship game.

Two of the best nights for Rhode Island College under Walsh's leadership don't appear in the numbers. In November of 2006, the Anchormen took down division I Iona College in an exhibition game 71-62, the first win over a division I team for RIC in over 30 years. They backed it up the following year by traveling to Holy Cross and taking down the Crusaders 61-60 on their home floor.

Prior to taking over the Rhode Island College program, Walsh was an assistant at Providence College for seven years. Well known as Tim Welsh's right-hand man on the bench, Walsh was a part of two NCAA Tournament teams and two NIT teams with the Friars. The 2004 Friars earned a number five seed in the NCAA Tournament, the highest seed in school history, and the Friars twice posted the most wins in Big East history while Walsh was on the bench.

Walsh started his coaching career while an undergraduate at Hamilton College, a division III power in central New York. He got his feet wet under legendary coach Tom Murphy at Hamilton, before moving on to be a graduate assistant at Iona College in New Rochelle, NY. Walsh joined Brad Holland at the University of San Diego for one season before returning East to join Welsh at Providence in April of 1998.

EPILOGUE

In late February of 2008, the year after our Elite Eight run, we were in Dartmouth, Massachusetts getting ready to take on UMass-Dartmouth in the Little East Title game. We had replaced our six seniors from the year before with some good young talent. We weren't as seasoned, but we had made it back to the championship game.

I spoke with John Weir and Tony Pierlioni, two of our graduated seniors from 2007, before the game. "These guys want to win today because they love to play, and they want to play in the NCAA Tournament. You guys wanted to win because you loved each other. You refused to let each other down. That's the difference."

That's what was *really* special about the 2007 team. The seniors had been through so much together over four years, including three different head coaches. They came to a program that two years before their arrival went 1-24. They won 11 games in their first year. They learned to play for one another above all else, and they absolutely refused to let their teammates down. They taught me how the bond that grows within a team that learns to play for one another can lead to something special.

The epitome of that approach was Kamari Williams. Kamari was clearly regarded as the best player in the program when I arrived—the league rookie of the year in 2004 and a first team all-LEC guard in 2005. With our change in approach, an influx of talent and Kamari dealing with some injuries his senior year, his role changed —as it did for others. All six of the seniors on our 2007 team were good enough to start for just about any other division III program, but only two of them started for us. Kamari came off the bench as a senior, playing only 13 minutes per game.

Kamari was the face of the program throughout his four years, a career that earned him induction into the RIC athletics hall of fame. You would think his status would make his decrease in minutes even tougher to handle, but instead Kamari became the unquestioned leader of our selfless approach. He wanted to play more, and I respected that. I wanted all of my players to feel that way. He would come talk to me in the office just about every week during the season, and he'd remind me how much he wanted to play and how he thought he could help the team. He'd ask me what he could do better to help us win, and I'd try and be as detailed as possible. But every time he'd leave my office, the last thing he would say was "I'm good, Coach. I want you to know that. I'm on board, and I just want to win." He was genuinely sincere. He never let his lack of playing time affect his approach. He would never let his teammates down.

Our program got devastating news when we learned in 2020 that Kamari had passed away at the age of 36. He had become a coach and a teacher in his hometown of Springfield, MA, having a significant impact on the youth of that city. I'd see him at a high school game or an AAU tournament, and he'd tell me stories about how his team wasn't listening to him, how they didn't get it. I'd open my eyes wide and raise one eyebrow looking at him, and we'd both laugh out loud, knowing he was once one of those very kids.

Kamari Williams may have had a bigger impact on the success of RIC basketball than any other player. When he arrived, RIC was one of the worst programs in the league. When he left, we were champions. His willingness to sacrifice and his commitment to his teammates became the soul of our program. It's impossible to quantify the impact he had on me as a young head coach.

Gone way too soon, Kamari William's legacy with his teammates and our program will last forever.

9 781733 692953